Fantastic Four

The Ultimate Guide

Fantastic Four

The Ultimate Guide

Tom DeFalco

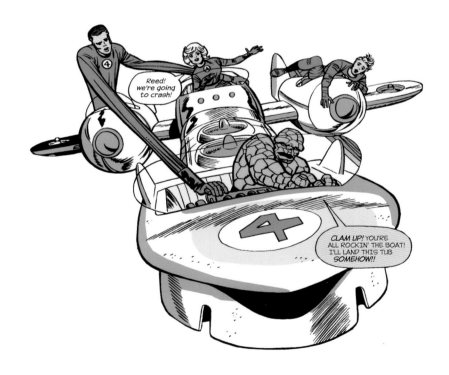

A DORLING KINDERSLEY BOOK

Contents

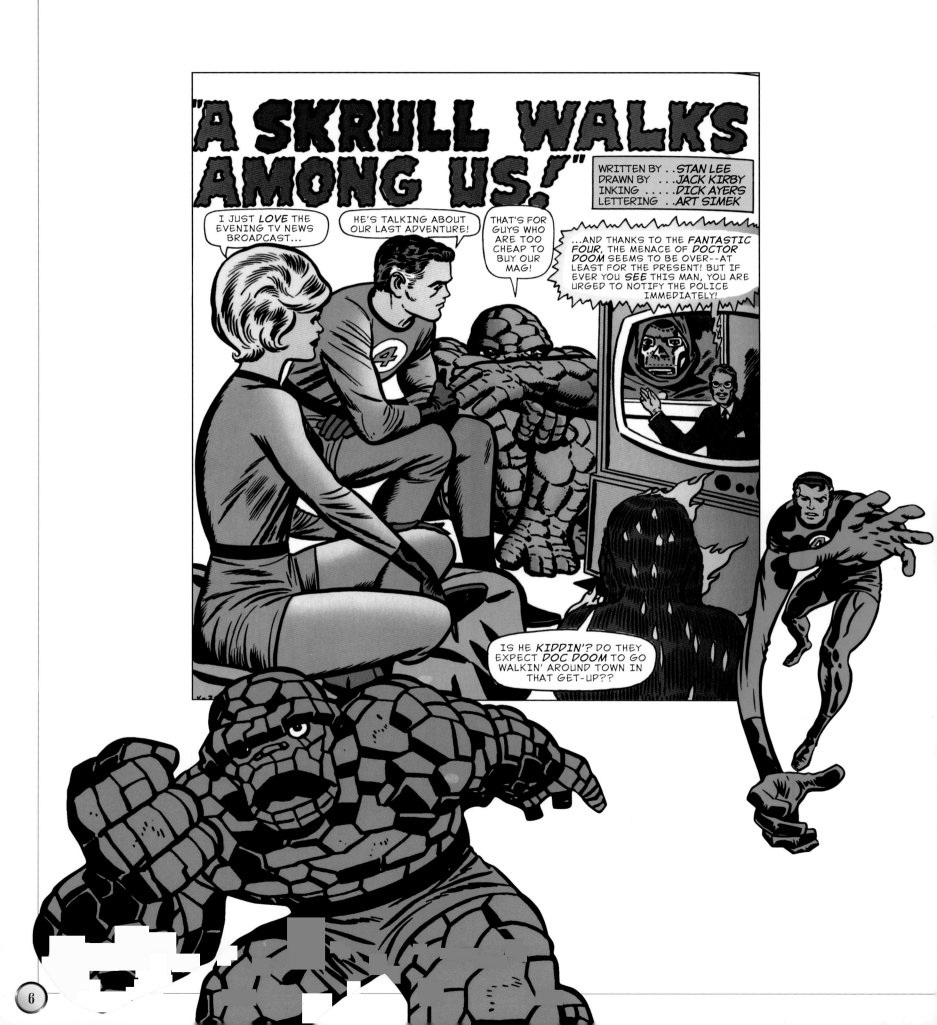

Why the "Fantastic Four?" Let me try to explain...

It was one of the toughest decisions of my comic-book career! I can't describe the agony, the sleepless nights, the mental torture—the fear of making the wrong choice.

But finally, I could put it off no longer. Staring artist Jack Kirby squarely in the eyes, I steeled my resolve, took a deep breath and firmly announced—

"We'll feature four heroes!"

There! The die was cast. The fateful number would be four. Not two or three or five or six, but four.

And what was the deep, philosophical, carefully-thought-out reason for that momentous decision? Simple—it sounded nice with the word "Fantastic!"

After producing countless assorted monster stories with the incredibly talented "King" Kirby, I had been given a new mission by the Powers That Be in our company. I was ordered to bestow the rare gift of Super Hero sagas onto the patiently waiting hordes of comic-book fandom.

Never had two guys been so excited by a project. I had the outline for the first story written and in Jack's hands before the day had ended. As for my "Master of the Pencil" partner, he was sketching designs for the characters seconds after I excitedly read him the story I had envisioned.

Y'know, as a writer, it's an amazing experience to collaborate with an artist, especially one as brilliant as Jack Kirby. Naturally, I had a conception in my mind of what the characters would look like and how they would move and act. But nothing could have prepared me for the shock I felt when I saw Jack's initial drawings. It was as though he had some uncanny power, some indescribable ability to get inside my skull, to grab the images that were swirling around in there and then, in some magical manner, to put them down on paper as if the drawings had come right from out of my head!

But that was only Phase One.

Now that our characters had been drawn and I could clearly see what they looked like, it was up to Jack and me to bring them to life, to make them seem like real people to the readers; even more than that—to make the fans care for them. That part of the job rested heavily on my shoulders. I knew our four featured players needed mannerisms, personality traits, and speech patterns that would make them interesting.

So I decided to make Reed, the leader, a guy who's so wrapped up in science and intelligence that he tends to overexplain things and to use big words, a trait that will always get under the skin of the more earthy Ben Grimm.

Johnny was the easiest. I'd make him a typical teenager, impatient, hot-blooded and overly impetuous. He likes girls and sports cars as much, and maybe more, than fighting the bad guys.

As for Sue, I didn't want her to be the typical girl who's always in danger, always having to be rescued by the hero. I wanted her to be an integral part of the team with equal power, courage, and grit.

Ben Grimm was my favorite. Although he's the one to whom Fate had dealt the most tragic hand, I wanted him to provide humor along with pathos. How well The Thing served that purpose, only you can judge.

I think I could talk about the FF for hours, but I haven't the heart to keep you from the good stuff for another minute. So welcome aboard, O True Believer, and f you enjoy the pages that follow as much as I did, you're gonna have a ball!

Excelsior!

Stan Lee

Introduction

There are certain pivotal moments that you never forget. Some people remember the day they graduated school, started a dream job, or met that very special person. For me and a lot of people like me the first time we picked up an issue of *Fantastic Four* is such a moment. I was 11 years old and already starting to outgrow comic books. My last few purchases hadn't exactly thrilled me. The heroes seemed more interested in protecting their secret identities than in being, well, *heroic*. More out of habit than interest, I walked to my local newsstand and studied the old-fashioned spinner rack where they kept the comics. I spotted two issues of a title that I'd never spotted before—*Fantastic Four #3* and #4. I still don't know what possessed me to pick up those comics, but I'm so glad I did. I didn't know it at the time, but I had just boarded the wildest roller coaster ride in the history of comics.

Fantastic Four #3 introduced me to Reed, Sue, Ben, and Johnny. I learned that they lived atop a skyscraper, and Sue even designed new costumes for everyone. (Ben, of course, shredded his a few pages later and never looked back.) They fought a super-powered hypnotist called the Miracle Man, who employed Godzilla-sized monsters and giant keys that transformed into automatic weapons. The team talked like real people and had plenty of attitude. So much attitude that the Human Torch quit at the end of the issue because he didn't like the way the Thing kept picking on him. He quit?!? My young mind reeled. Super Heroes didn't quit. It just wasn't done. At least not until *Fantastic Four* came along.

It seemed like *Fantastic Four* broke new ground every issue. We learned that Super Heroes faced problems finding parking spaces for their super-vehicles, and they could even go bankrupt. We met the Sub-Mariner, who fell in love with Sue, and we were shocked when she actually seemed interested. (Hey, wasn't she supposed to be in love with Reed?!) We cheered when Ben started dating Alicia and trembled when Doctor Doom unleashed his next deadly plan. We were frustrated when Reed couldn't find a way to cure the Thing, and we smiled whenever Ben met the Yancy Street Gang or mentioned Aunt Petunia.

The team took us into the past with Blackbeard the pirate, across the galaxy to Planet X, up to the Blue Area of the Moon, down into the Micro-World, and to the bottom of the deep blue sea. We battled Skrulls, diabolical duos, deadly androids, and the Incredible Hulk. We faced the menace of a world-eater and explored the anti-matter universe of the Negative Zone.

We saw the FF lose their powers and later battle for the Baxter Building. We saw the Thing crush Doom's hands and witnessed the noble sacrifice of Franklin Storm. We were present for the wedding of Sue and Reed and celebrated the birth of their son a few years later. We watched Johnny fall in love with Crystal and sympathized when Ben feared he was losing Alicia to the Silver Surfer.

If you don't know what I'm talking about, just keep turning the pages. This book will introduce you to the wonder that is *The World's Greatest Comic Magazine*! You will meet the team and learn about their powers, their friends, their enemies, their triumphs, and their tragedies. You'll get an overview of their history and of the creative people who helped produce their monthly adventures. If you're already familiar with everyone's favorite foursome, you will revisit old friends and remember times past.

I have always believed that the golden age of comics is the age you were when you first started reading. Please sit back and enjoy….

Fantastic Four Origins

FIRST FLARE

People didn't know what to make of the flare that suddenly appeared in the sky over Central City, California, and feared it signaled an alien invasion!

REED **R**ICHARDS always dreamed of exploring the stars. The son of Nathaniel and Evelyn Richards, Reed was a child genius and he excelled in science and mathematics. His father was a brilliant physicist and his mother died when he was seven years old. Already taking college-level courses by the time he was 14, Reed studied at many different colleges and universities, and gained numerous degrees. Whilst at State University, he shared a room with football star Ben Grimm. They became best friends and Reed shared his dream with Ben of building a starship someday. Ben, who wanted to become a pilot, promised to fly it. Reed never forgot Ben's offer and spent the next few years working on his designs for the ship.

Journey into the unknown

Ben joined the United States Air Force and became a skilled test pilot and astronaut. After leaving the military, he was shocked to learn that Reed had managed to build a starship, using government funding and his own family fortune. Just prior to the project's completion, the government threatened to close it down. This infuriated Reed and motivated him to take the spaceship on an impromptu test flight. Ben objected, fearing that the ship didn't have adequate shielding to protect them from cosmic rays. However, Reed's fiancée, Susan Storm, persuaded Ben to change his mind and so Reed, Ben, Sue, and her teenage brother Johnny embarked on a journey that was to change their lives forever.

IF YOU WANT TO FLY TO THE STARS, THEN *YOU* PILOT THE SHIP! COUNT *ME* OUT!

YOU *KNOW* WE HAVEN'T DONE ENOUGH RESEARCH INTO THE EFFECT OF COSMIC RAYS! THEY MIGHT KILL US ALL OUT IN SPACE!

LADIES FIRST

Sue was the first one to exhibit special powers when she suddenly disappeared before everyone's eyes.

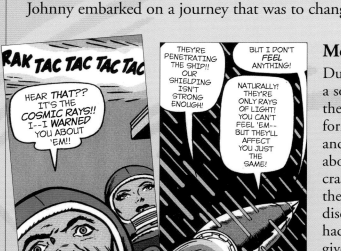

RAK TAC TAC TAC TAC

HEAR *THAT*?? IT'S THE *COSMIC RAYS!!* I--I *WARNED* YOU ABOUT 'EM!!

THEY'RE PENETRATING THE SHIP!! OUR SHIELDING ISN'T STRONG ENOUGH!

BUT I DON'T *FEEL* ANYTHING!

NATURALLY! THEY'RE ONLY RAYS OF LIGHT! YOU CAN'T FEEL 'EM-- BUT THEY'LL AFFECT YOU JUST THE SAME!

More than human

During the group's voyage, a solar flare bombarded the ship with an unknown form of cosmic radiation, and they were forced to abort the mission. The ship crash-landed on Earth, and the four adventurers soon discovered that the radiation had altered their bodies and given them fantastic powers. Sue developed the ability to turn completely invisible, and Ben transformed into a thick-skinned, heavily muscled creature. Reed's body had become as stretchy as a piece of elastic, and Johnny grew hotter and hotter until his body burst into flames and he became a Human Torch.

SOMEHOW THE COSMIC RAYS HAVE ALTERED YOUR ATOMIC STRUCTURE...MAKING YOU GROW INVISIBLE!

SIS! I CAN'T SEE YOU AT *ALL* ANY MORE!

HOW... HOW LONG WILL IT *LAST*?

JOHNNY! WHAT *IS* IT? WHAT'S HAPPENING TO YOU?

I DON'T KNOW, SIS! MY BODY FEELS HOT-- LIKE IT'S ON FIRE!! I--I FEEL LIKE I'M BURNING UP!!

This man, this monster

Ben was furious with Reed for not listening to him about the shielding. He lost his temper and tried to flatten his former roommate! Ben was so angry that it took him a while to realize that his body was undergoing a spectacular transformation. His skin was turning orange and rocklike in appearance, and he had gained superhuman strength. Ben became depressed when he realized that, unlike his friends, he couldn't return to normal. The others had gained super-powers, but he had become a monster… a thing.

AN ELASTIC MAN

As he tried to calm Ben down, Reed discovered that he could now stretch his limbs to astounding lengths, like a human rubber band!

Mole Man

Deep below the city streets lives the Mole Man. Almost blind since childhood and branded a misfit, Mole Man eventually rejected humanity and went in search of the center of the Earth. On an island in the Bermuda Triangle, he discovered a cavern that led him to an underground world he named Subterranea. Here the outcast found refuge amidst the strange monsters and semi-human creatures who resided there and soon became their ruler. In his dank and dingy realm Mole Man developed a "radar-sense" that allowed him to navigate his way around and was soon devising fiendish plans, involving his army of monsters, to punish the surface world for the way it had treated him.

MONSTERS

One of Mole Man's schemes was to steal every power plant on the planet and then unleash his giant monsters against mankind. Luckily, the FF were there to thwart his evil plan.

From tragedy to triumph

It took time for the enormity of their situation to finally hit them. Each of them now had more power than anyone had ever possessed, and they all pledged to use their abilities for the good of mankind. The four adventurers formed a legal corporation and set up offices in New York City, as if they were starting a new business together. As the Fantastic Four, they safeguard the planet from extraterrestrial threats and earthly super-menaces that are too powerful for conventional peacekeepers. The team offers its services without charge and is funded by the patents on Reed's various inventions and scientific discoveries.

Mr. Fantastic   Reed Richards

REED **R**ICHARDS was a child prodigy who grew up to become a scientific and mathematical mastermind with a genius for technological invention. Charismatic and a born leader—almost no problem is too tough for Reed to solve. And he knows it, adopting the alias Mr. Fantastic as his *nom de guerre* in the Fantastic Four, the Super Hero group he proudly leads against the forces of evil. Mr. Fantastic's mental abilities are amazing enough, yet they pale in comparison with his physical powers. Exposure to a massive dose of radiation during the trial run of his starship dramatically altered his molecular structure. His strength remained that of a normal man, but his body became endowed with incredible elasticity and malleability.

Elastic fantastic

Reed soon came to realize that he could will his body to take on any shape his imagination conceived—bending it, condensing it, expanding it, or stretching it. Mr. Fantastic has now achieved total mastery over his physical powers: in a matter of seconds, he can compress his body into any solid shape of a volume no greater than 1.7 cubic feet or spread his body out in different directions, turning it into a living canopy, a parachute, or a thin-walled enclosure. He can flatten his body until it is no wider than a sheet of paper or extend his neck, torso, and limbs 1,500 feet without discomfort. His body's internal organs and respiration and circulatory systems remain totally unaffected by his changes in shape. However, the greater the distance he stretches himself, the weaker he becomes. Just as he can alter his shape in seconds, so he can revert to his normal human form in mere moments.

SUSAN STORM

Reed first met his future wife, Susan Storm (Invisible Woman), when he was a young student at Columbia University. She was his landlady's 12-year-old niece!

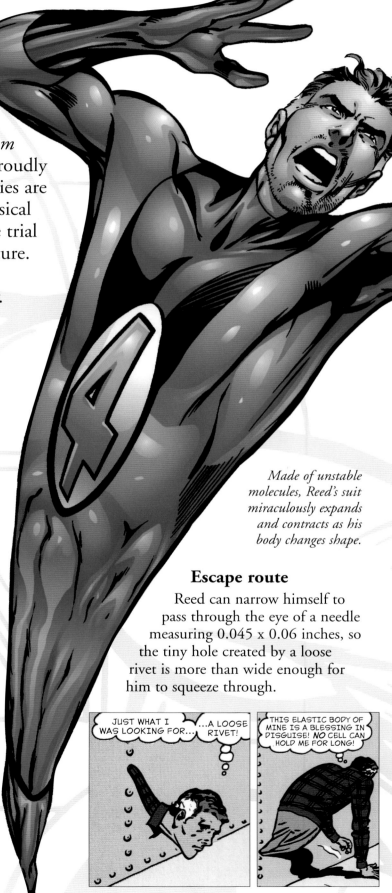

Made of unstable molecules, Reed's suit miraculously expands and contracts as his body changes shape.

Escape route

Reed can narrow himself to pass through the eye of a needle measuring 0.045 x 0.06 inches, so the tiny hole created by a loose rivet is more than wide enough for him to squeeze through.

Spring loaded

Mr. Fantastic coiled his body into a human spring to propel the Thing in pursuit of the Frightful Four. The Thing hurtled into the air and crashed onto the villains' spaceship. Soon it was "clobberin' time" for the Fantastic Four's evil rivals!

Underwater camouflage

On the trail of the evil Attuma and his undersea army, the Fantastic Four had to pass by an enemy patrol unnoticed. When all hope seemed lost, Mr. Fantastic changed his body into the form of a giant ray and transported his teammates safely past the enemy patrol. Just as the weight of carrying the others was beginning to prove too much for the Fantastic Four's leader to bear, the Thing bailed out and singlehandedly captured one of Attuma's deep-sea tanks.

BULLETPROOF

Reed's unique molecular structure means that no bullet or shell can harm him. His body absorbs the energy of a projectile and expels it with deadly force.

Knockout punch

A lack of super-strength proves no barrier to Mr. Fantastic's effectiveness as a hand-to-hand combatant. His scientific expertise enables him to supplement his amazing reach, speed, and flexibility with awesome hitting power. Fitted with concussive knuckle-dusters, Mr. Fantastic's two fists pack a pile-driving punch—enough to put a dent in Annihilus's armored jaw and knock the insectoid senseless!

Invisible Woman
Susan Storm Richards

WITHOUT SUE RICHARDS, there would probably be no Fantastic Four! Time after time, she has acted as the group's peacemaker when the other members have fallen out. When Reed loses patience with Johnny, or when the Thing's resentment against Reed for not curing him boils over, Sue is always there with consoling words. Sue and her younger brother Johnny were brought up in a comfortable, loving home in Long Island until tragedy struck when their mother died in a car crash and their father was sent to prison. At age 12, while staying at her aunt's rooming house in Manhattan, Sue met Reed Richards and developed a crush on him. However, the foundations had been laid for a lasting friendship that would one day become love and marriage.

Sue felt that the Fantastic Four needed distinctive costumes and outfitted all the members—except the Thing, who refused to wear a "fool outfit."

Love and invisibility

Years later, Sue moved to California, dreaming of Hollywood stardom. She met up once more with Reed Richards, who had become an aeronautical engineer, and the two fell in love. When she found out that Reed was about to launch a starship with Ben Grimm as pilot, she insisted that she and Johnny should also be among the crew. Caught in a radiation storm along with the others, she discovered that she could turn invisible at will and became a member of the Fantastic Four.

Powers of projection

First taking the alias Invisible Girl and later changing it to Invisible Woman, Sue soon realized that the mutagenic changes the radiation had caused went much further than simply an ability to disappear in a crisis. She discovered that she could make others invisible as well and also that she possessed the ability to manipulate cosmic energy with her mind. Among other things, this power enabled her to create invisible fields that could withstand considerable amounts of force. One of the most spectacular early demonstrations of Invisible Woman's psionic skills occurred when Mr. Fantastic and the Thing lay at the mercy of the Sentry. Before the merciless automaton could deliver a death-dealing blow, quick-thinking Sue concealed her partners from sight and shielded them with a force field.

INVISIBILITY
Sue's amazing powers of invisibility could not preserve her from the clutches of the Mole Man's minions, who were all virtually blind.

SOLID SHAPES
One of Invisible Woman's most useful psionic powers is her ability to create simple solid shapes in moments. As if by magic, she creates a see-through bobsleigh so that she and Reed can speed down a hill and make it back to their interdimensional portal.

Keeping the peace

Sue is quick to intervene when the team starts squabbling, surrounding the Thing with an invisible force field strong enough to stop his violent attacks. Sue also possesses the power to make other beings or things invisible, and she can appear to fly by projecting columns of psionic force to keep her airborne.

A fantastic family

Sue married her sweetheart Reed Richards in a ceremony attended by many heroes. The birth of a son, Franklin, named after Sue's late father, brought the couple even closer together. Sue and Reed later had a daughter. Doctor Doom helped at the birth—as long as the baby was called Valeria after his first and only love.

Weapons of the mind

She may not be any stronger than a normal, physically fit woman, but Sue can be a formidable adversary when her anger is roused. She certainly got her message across to Doctor Doom when he snatched her son, Franklin. She created a stream of invisible flying grappling hooks with her mind that attacked the villain's brain.

CIRCUS TRICK

Johnny Storm is a natural show-off and loves soaking up the applause. Generating and juggling fireballs, while creating flaming rings and balancing on one arm on a high wire, is nothing to him! He is even able to fly on a cloud of hydrogen emitted by his plasma fire (below).

Human Torch Johnny Storm

HOT-HEADED and filled with boundless energy, Jonathan "Johnny" Storm adds youthful enthusiasm and rebel cool to the Fantastic Four—in addition to a range of incredible, fiery super-powers. He is Sue Storm's younger brother and was only nine when their mother was killed and he had to endure the pain of losing a parent. Johnny became obsessed with motor vehicles and, by the age of 16, was a master mechanic and a daredevil hot-rodder. He accompanied his sister on the fateful first voyage of Reed Richards' starship. When it was hit by a freak radiation storm, every molecule in his body was spectacularly altered.

Fire and passion

Back on Earth, Johnny found that he could generate fiery plasma from his body. Taking the name the Human Torch, he joined Reed Richards' team of champions, the Fantastic Four. His attempts to lead a normal life, finishing high school and blending in with the community, proved hopeless, and he and Sue, the Invisible Woman, were soon ensconced in the team's headquarters in New York's Baxter Building. Johnny married Alicia Masters, whom the Thing also loved, causing a bitter rift within the team for a while until they discovered that Alicia was actually a shape-changing Skrull spy. The real Alicia had been spirited away to the Skrull's homeworld and was duly rescued by the team. Alicia still loved the Thing, and Johnny embarked on a series of affairs of the heart.

CANDLE POWER

The Human Torch and the Thing have a very competitive relationship— the Thing is jealous of Johnny's good looks and cleverness and pours scorn on his flashy style. However, even the super-strong Thing has to admit that the Human Torch's explosive "candle punch" is hot stuff!

AND EVEN IF YOUR SPEARS ARE TIPPED IN A POTION WHICH WILL HARM MY FLAMING BODY, FIRST YOU HAVETA FIGURE OUT WHICH OF THESE FLAMING IMAGES I CAN CREATE IS THE *REAL ME!*

In control

Johnny can generate fiery plasma of about 780 degrees Fahrenheit from all or part of his body at will, without harm to himself or his clothes (which are composed of unstable molecules). He can maintain this heat intensity for up to 16 hours. For short periods, he can increase the heat he emits to what he terms "nova flame" levels. He can also release all his body's energy in a devastating "nova-burst" explosion.

Flame on!

The Human Torch lacks superhuman strength. However, one of Johnny's many amazing abilities is to create flaming duplicates of himself that turn him into a one-man army!

Flames extend up to 5 inches from Johnny's body.

The Human Torch can absorb vast amounts of heat energy into his body without coming to any harm—as these soldiers from the Brüm Nebula rapidly realized.

PUTTING OUT THE TORCH

To produce fire, the Torch needs oxygen and so can be extinguished in low air-pressure or a vacuum. Johnny's flames can also be briefly doused by large amounts of water or smothered by fire-fighting materials such as sand, foam, and fire-resistant chemicals.

Fearsome fire

The Human Torch's powers are immense and extremely dangerous in the wrong hands, as the Fantastic Four discovered when Johnny's body was temporarily taken over by Doctor Doom's spirit. The evil sorcerer had complete control of Johnny's mighty arsenal of fire-formed weapons and directed each attack with deadly accuracy.

HEY -- DON'T! LEGGO!

S'MATTER? YA WANT OUT, DON'T YA?

HERE! HAVE A FREE RIDE, COMPLIMENTS OF *THE THING*!

GANGWAY!

UNHAPPY LANDINGS

Ben Grimm, alias The Thing, is as bighearted as he is tough. He has a rough-and-ready sense of humor—in fact, sometimes troublemakers find his humor rather too rough!

The Thing
Benjamin Jacob Grimm

FATE GAVE Ben the name Grimm, and grim has often been his fate! He was born and raised on Yancy Street in Manhattan's tough, poverty-stricken Lower East Side. His father was an alcoholic, and his older brother Daniel was killed in a street fight.

At age 18, Ben succeeded Daniel as leader of the Yancy Street Gang and seemed locked into a world of petty crime. However, Ben's life turned around when his parents died and he was adopted by his Uncle Jake, a doctor. After initial opposition, Ben responded positively to his uncle's care. He left the gang and completed high school. His impressive physique made him a star of the football team, and he later won a football scholarship to Empire State University.

Monstrous mutation

At university, Ben's roommate was Reed Richards. The tough, no-nonsense Ben Grimm and the brilliant, wealthy science student Reed Richards became firm friends. Years later, Reed asked Ben, by now an experienced test pilot and astronaut, to join the crew of his prototype starship. Ben pointed out that the ship's radiation shield might not be powerful enough, but Reed was determined to test his starship anyway. Caught in a powerful radiation storm in space, pilot Grimm was forced to abort the flight and return to Earth. As with the other crew members, the radiation blast had extraordinary effects on Ben's molecular structure. His skin mutated into thick, heavy, orange scales; his musculature increased immensely; he became superhumanly strong and powerful. At first, Ben could sometimes change back to his original form, but all too soon, he would revert to the monstrous body of The Thing.

YOU'VE GOT YOURSELF A NEW ROOMIE, RICHARDS! THE NAME'S BEN GRIMM! I FIGURE I'LL BE MORE LAUGHS THAN THE NUT WHO JUST FLEW OUTTA HERE!

BEN GRIMM, THE *TOUCHDOWN KING?* GLAD TO HAVE YOU, BIG FELLA!

Keeping fit

Reed Richards has devised a state-of-the art gym in the Fantastic Four's base in New York's Baxter Building. The gym's high-tech weight machines help to ensure that Ben keeps his massive muscles toned.

DON'T GO 'WAY... YA AIN'T SEEN NOTHIN' YET!!

BAM!

BAM!

The Thing's skin can withstand armor-piercing shells and extreme heat and cold.

> BEN ALWAYS LOVED TO HEAR ME PLAY AND SING!

Alicia and the Thing

Sculptress Alicia Masters is the love of Ben's life. Being blind, she is not put off by his grotesque appearance. Ben once believed that Alicia had fallen in love with Johnny Storm. Broken-hearted and wracked with jealousy, Ben left the Fantastic Four for a spell. Ben also worries about Alicia's close friendship with the Silver Surfer.

> DON'T WORRY, SONNY BOY... I'M NOT GONNA SPOIL YOUR PRETTY FEATURES! I'LL JUST ROUGH YOU UP A LITTLE... TEACH YOU WHO'S *BOSS*, ONCE AND FOR ALL!

> DON'T TRY IT, THING! I'M *WARNIN'* YOU!

> YOU'RE WARNING ME??!!

> WHY, I'LL...

> HEY!! WHAT'S HAPPENIN'?!! I - I'M CHANGING!

> BUT SUDDENLY A LONG, PLIABLE *ARM* REACHES OUT, GRABBING THE STEEL - SINEWED WRIST OF BEN GRIMM LIKE A COILED *SNAKE* ...

> HOLD IT, BEN... *HOLD IT!* YOU DON'T KNOW WHAT YOU'RE DOING, FELLA!

> STAY OUTTA THIS, STRETCH! IT AIN'T NONE OF *YOUR* BUSINESS... SO LEGGO!!

The Thing needs no pressurized suit to survive in space or in the ocean depths.

> I'M *MAKING* IT MY BUSINESS, BEN!

> ALICIA PHONED US... SICK WITH *WORRY!* SHE *BEGGED* US TO FIND YOU... TO BRING YOU TO YOUR *SENSES.* IF YOU'VE ANY LEFT!

> WE'VE BEEN *SEARCHING* FOR YOU IN THAT POLICE HELICOPTER!

> NOW *SIMMER DOWN* AND LET ME *EXPLAIN..!*

> EXPLAIN *WHAT??!*

> I'M *HUMAN* AGAIN!! I'M BEN GRIMM AGAIN!! AT LAST! *AT LAST!*

Reed and Susan calm Ben down during one of his jealous episodes.

Trapped in a monster's body

From time to time, either by accident or the scientific experiments of Reed Richards, Ben has returned to normal. However, the effects are short-lived, and his joy rapidly turns to dismay as his body swells and his skin reverts to the consistency of rock. Although his hide is virtually impenetrable, Ben is still susceptible to illness and stress. His intelligence level and basic personality are unaffected by his mutation into the Thing. When beating up the bad guys, his favorite catchprase is, "It's clobberin' time!"

Fantastic Family

IF **THERE** is a single trait that distinguishes the Fantastic Four from all the other teams of super-powered adventurers, it is the fact that the FF is also a family. Reed, Ben, Sue, and Johnny were bound together long before they entered the starship and gained their superhuman powers. Reed met Ben in college, and they became lifelong friends. Sue fell in love with Reed while he was still attending Columbia University. Johnny always knew his sister's fiancé was destined for greatness and went along for the ride. The FF also have an extended family tree....

Reed and Sue were finally married in a public ceremony, attended by the Avengers and the X-Men. Stan Lee and Jack Kirby tried to crash the party but were ejected.

■ MARRIED
══ CHILDREN

Nathanial Richards
Nathanial became warlord of an alternate Earth. On his return to real Earth, he turned Franklin into a teen.

Evelyn Richards
A former teacher, Evelyn gave up her career when she married Nathanial. She died after a long illness when Reed was only seven years old.

Franklin Storm
A world-renowned surgeon, Franklin turned to gambling after he failed to save his wife's life. Unable to pay his debts, he fought with a loan shark and was convicted of his manslaughter. In prison, Franklin was kidnapped by Skrulls and sacrificed himself to save Sue and Johnny.

Mary Storm
Mary Storm was fatally injured in a car accident on the way to a dinner in honor of her husband. Not only was Franklin driving the car, but he operated on Mary in a desperate attempt to save her life. After the death of her mother and the imprisonment of her father, Susan took charge of raising her younger brother, Johnny.

Huntara
Half-sister of Reed from an alternate Earth, Huntara is Guardian of the Sacred Timestreams.

Reed Richards
A former child prodigy, Reed is the leader and a founding member of the FF.

Susan Storm
Susan first fell in love with Reed when he was a student.

Johnny Storm
"Hothead" Johnny loves fast cars and beautiful women.

Lyja (Skrull)
A disguised Skrull, Lyja pretended to be Alicia Masters and married Johnny.

Torus Storm

In the same timeline, Torus becomes Super-Storm.

Rachael Summers, Phoenix

In various possible timelines, Franklin is fated to marry the daughter of Scott "Cyclops" Summer and Jean "Phoenix."

The Thing's closest relatives:

Uncle Jake

A successful physician, Jacob Grimm provided a home and a family for his teenage nephew Ben after the deaths of his parents.

Aunt Petunia

A student nurse, Aunt Petunia (Penny) raised Ben with Uncle Jake.

Benjamin Jacob Grimm

The ever lovin' blue-eyed Thing.

TWINS

In at least one possible future, Ben marries Sharon Ventura, and they have twins. Jacob inherits Ben's Thing-like appearance and Alyce gains the power to manipulate energy. Sharon and Ben later divorced.

Ben's twins

Jacob and Alyce Grimm.

Franklin Richards

Possessing enormous telekinetic and telepathic potential, Franklin is destined to become the super-adventurer known as Psi-Lord.

Hyperstorm

Valeria Richards

The second child of Reed and Sue, Val has yet to exhibit any superhuman abilities.

ALTERNATE TIMELINE

Rama-Tut, Kang, Immortus, and the Scarlet Centurion are alternate timeline versions of the same man, who believed himself to be a descendant of Dr. Doom. However, his ancestor is actually Nathanial Richards.

HYPERSTORM

In one possible future, Hyperstorm is the only child of Franklin and Rachael Summers. After inheriting the telepathic and telekinetic powers of his father and the virtually limitless power of his mother, he conquers the entire known universe and becomes the great enemy that Nathanial Richards has sworn to destroy.

WHO... WHO ARE YOU?!

I FEAR THAT YOU ARE NOT QUITE PREPARED TO LEARN MY TRUE IDENTITY, MRS. RICHARDS.

SUFFICE IT TO SAY THAT I AM KNOWN BY MANY NAMES ON COUNTLESS WORLDS. THE ONE I MOST PREFER IS... *HYPERSTORM!*

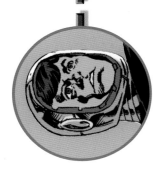

Kristoff Vernard

Nathanial once indicated that he was Kristoff's father, but this has never been confirmed.

Rama-Tut

Kang

Immortus

Scarlet Centurion

Fantastic Friends

Willie Lumpkin has no powers, except for a good heart and an ability to wiggle his ears!

BEING PART of a Super Hero team, battling evil and dazzling the world with your powers sounds great, but it has a downside: you will be hounded by the paparazzi and attract the envy, even the fear, of sections of the public. Living outside normal society, the Fantastic Four have learned to rely on a small circle of friends. Some of these allies are ordinary folk, others heroes in their own right—but all are highly valued by the FF.

MY NAME'S BILLIE. I'M YOUR MAIL MAN, I MEAN, WOMAN.

THE LUMPKINS

Mailman Willie Lumpkin's life was transformed when the Fantastic Four moved into the Baxter Building, on his route. Willie has done the team some good turns, even saving them from the Mad Thinker. When he retired, his niece Billie replaced him as the FF's favorite mail carrier.

Spider-Man

One of the most famous of the Fantastic Four's friends is the amazing web-slinging, wall-climbing Spider-Man. He is Johnny's best friend and has often been called upon to use his superhuman strength and agility—and, of course, his spider-sense—to come to the aid of the FF.

YOU ARE WEARING A HIGHLY EVOLVED *SYMBIOTE*-- A SENTIENT BEING WHICH HAS ATTACHED ITSELF TO YOU BOTH MENTALLY AND PHYSICALLY!

YOU MEAN... *IT'S ALIVE?!*

POSSESSED

Mr. Fantastic realizes why Spider-Man feels utterly exhausted and is having terrible nightmares. Spidey's new suit is alive and taking the wall-crawler on weird nighttime adventures, of which he has no memory on waking.

Saving Spidey

Spider-Man has cause to be grateful to his friends. Spidey tore his costume to shreds during a battle with the tyrannical Beyonder and found a strange, alien machine that supplied him with a new, black one. Reed Richards soon realized that this alien costume was fast turning Spider-Man into its puppet!

Agatha Harkness

Once the leader of the witch colony of New Salem, Agatha became Franklin Richards' governess, protecting him with her magic. She fell foul of her son, Nicholas Scratch, and was sentenced to death by her own grandchildren— the evil Salem's Seven—for daring to consort with the outside world.

A heroic occasion

The Fantastic Four remain close friends with the Avengers and the X-Men. Both Super Hero teams were guests at Reed Richards and Sue Storm's engagement party.

ALYSSA MOY

Before Reed Richards fell in love with Sue Storm, Alyssa Moy was a close companion. They first met in college, though whether they had any romantic involvement is not known. She is highly intelligent and resourceful, a born explorer and adventurer.

Alicia Masters

Blindness only intensified Alicia's compassion for others and her own artistic gifts—her sculptures have brought her worldwide fame. She fell in love with the Thing, being able to "see" the kind heart that lay beneath his rough exterior. She also had a close relationship with the Silver Surfer.

Wingfoot

The son of decathlon champion Will Wingfoot, Native American Wyatt Wingfoot became friends with Johnny Storm at Metro College, New York City. His tracking skills, bravery, athleticism, and ability with animals have proved useful on several FF adventures.

Alysande Stuart

Given protection by the Fantastic Four and a job as Franklin Richards' nanny, Alysande Stuart, alias Caledonia, champion of ancient Scotland, is willing to lay down her life for the team.

The friendship between Spider-Man and the Torch is tense at times, but deep down their bond is strong. When the FF's popularity plummeted temporarily, Spider-Man helped his crestfallen friend win back public acclaim, although Johnny's self-pitying tested his patience!

Fill-in FFers

MEMBERSHIP of other super-groups, such as the Avengers and the X-Men, is constantly changing, but the Fantastic Four still has its original teammates. Individual members may have taken the occasional leave of absence over the years, or even quit for periods of time, but they always returned. However, when a temporary vacancy does arise in the Fantastic Four, there is always someone ready to take the job.

CRYSTAL'S POWERS

Crystal can direct just one elemental force at a time, and she can only use her powers for about an hour before she needs to rest.

Crystal, the exquisite elemental

Crystal has twice served as a substitute member of the Fantastic Four. She is an Inhuman who has the ability to psionically manipulate earth, wind, water, and fire. She can create seismic tremors, control the flow of water, ignite fires, and generate winds.

MAGNIFICENT MANE

Medusa's hair is super-strong and can lift nearly two tons. She can also employ it to do complex tasks like shoveling cards or picking locks.

Medusa

Though she was a founding member of the Frightful Four, Crystal's older sister, Medusa, also did a brief stint on the Fantastic Four. Medusa possesses a head of long, thick hair that is the source of her power. It obeys her mental commands, and she is only limited by her imagination. She can rotate it in a fanlike manner to generate fierce winds or use it to bind her enemies. It can also lift her to the top of tall buildings or cushion a fall.

IN THE FAMILY

A blood transfusion from her cousin, Dr. Robert Bruce Banner (who is secretly the Incredible Hulk), gave Jennifer Walters the ability to transform into the She-Hulk.

40¢ 1 FEB

MARVEL COMICS GROUP

THE SAVAGE **SHE-HULK** #1 COLLECTOR'S ITEM ISSUE!

STAN LEE PROUDLY PRESENTS: THE SHE-HULK LIVES!

Sensational She-Hulk

While the Hulk and Banner usually have distinct personalities, the She-Hulk has Jennifer Walter's mind and personality. She isn't quite as strong as her cousin but can still lift 75 tons without too much effort. While working with the FF, Jennifer met and started dating Wyatt Wingfoot.

The astonishing Ant-Man

Scott Lang was an electronics expert who briefly turned to crime and broke into the home of Dr. Henry Pym, the original Ant-Man. Scott stole Pym's Ant-Man costume and shrinking canisters and used them to rescue a kidnapped doctor. When he later tried to return the stolen items, Pym offered to let Scott become the new Ant-Man. Aside from his scientific expertise, the Ant-Man can also shrink to the size of an ant while retaining his normal human strength.

Power Man

When the team needed someone to fill in for the Thing, Reed Richards hired Luke Cage. While not as strong as Ben Grimm, Power Man does possess super-strength and steel-hard skin. Bullets bounce off him, and his fists can shatter a concrete wall. He is also a self-taught street fighter and a superb athlete. While working with the FF, Power Man fell under the Puppet Master's spell and turned against the team.

THE SHE-THING

While on a mission to space, Sharon Ventura was accidentally exposed to cosmic rays and mutated into a female version of the Thing. She now possessed super-strength and was powerful enough to hold her own against the She-Hulk.

BEN, WHAT'S **HAPPENED** TO ME --?!!

Ms. Marvel

Sharon Ventura was the only child of an army officer who wanted a son. Trying to live up to her father's expectations, she studied martial arts and became a gifted athlete. She also mastered mountain climbing, skydiving, ski-jumping, and scuba diving. Sharon first met the Thing while he was on vacation from the FF, working as a professional wrestler. She eventually underwent a process that artificially enhanced her strength, speed, and endurance. Sharon designed a costume and began to call herself Ms. Marvel. After she helped the Fantastic Four defeat Diablo, Ben invited her to join the team.

Ms. Marvel is an expert in martial arts, including Tae Kwon Do.

Headquarters & Hardware

THE FOUNDING members of the Fantastic Four are the owners of a private corporation that specializes in scientific research. Fantastic Four, Inc. is financed by the profits from the patents on those inventions that Reed Richards chooses to share with the public. Many of his developments—like the unstable molecules used in their jumpsuits—are designed to help the team protect the Earth.

ROBERTA
The FF's robotic receptionist can do many things at one time and is programmed in martial arts.

Security first

The team's first base of operations was in the top five floors of the original Baxter Building in midtown Manhattan. Reed outfitted the roof with security monitors that showed the roof and recorded anything that approached it. A computerized security system guarded the interior, using retina scans to identify anyone who entered the building. A team of robots would automatically be activated to subdue intruders.

Changing headquarters

The original Baxter Building was ripped from its foundations and hurled into space, where it was destroyed by Kristoff Vernard. While staying at Avengers Mansion, the FF constructed a new headquarters on the original site. Four Freedoms Plaza was a 45-story office building that contained four more stories for their headquarters. When another team commandeered the building, the FF briefly moved into their warehouse storage facility at Pier 4. Four Freedoms Plaza was destroyed and a new version of the Baxter Building now stands in its place.

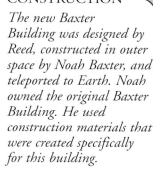

CONSTRUCTION
The new Baxter Building was designed by Reed, constructed in outer space by Noah Baxter, and teleported to Earth. Noah owned the original Baxter Building. He used construction materials that were created specifically for this building.

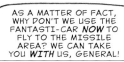

Flying Bathtub

Reed designed the first Fantasti-car because he wanted a vehicle that could travel around Manhattan and would be easy to park. Powered by rechargeable batteries, it is essentially a flying electric golf cart that uses electromagnetic waves to float. It can reach a top speed of nearly 50 mph.

Fantasti-crafts

As the team expanded its operations, Reed realized they needed a vehicle with much greater speed and cruising range. Working with Johnny Storm, he built an improved Fantasti-car that was equipped with bulletproof windshields that roll into place at the flick of a switch. For quick jaunts, the team also has an airjet-cycle that is propelled by compressed cushions of air. Ben even has an individual jet-cycle.

FLARE GUNS

Each team member is equipped with a wireless communications link and has an emergency flare gun. The flares can be seen anywhere in the city and are used to instantly gather the entire FF. The mayor and chief of police have also been given flare guns.

THE FANTASTI-CAR

Designed to function both as a team vehicle or to separate into four distinct flying machines, the original Fantasti-car can easily hover 40 stories above the ground.

Pogo-Planes and time travel

While Reed invents most of the FF's technology, he also uses devices secured from their enemies. For quick trips around the world, the FF have a Pogo-Plane that has vertical takeoff and landing abilities. They also have a captured Skrull starship that they use for galactic travel. A time platform and space/time sled are available for trips into alternate time eras or dimensions.

SIXTIES

The Fantastic Four in the 1960s

According to legend, *The Fantastic Four* (and the entire Marvel Universe) were born on a golf course. Martin Goodman, who owned the company that would eventually become known as Marvel Comics, was playing golf one day with Jack Liebowitz, who ran the comic-book publisher that would become DC Comics. Liebowitz happened to mention that his best-selling title was *The Justice League of America*, the story of a team of Super Heroes. Goodman told his editor and chief writer, Stan Lee, to come up with a super-team that they could publish. Stan was not too keen on the idea at first. Goodman had already published and abandoned Super Hero comics in the 1940s and 1950s. Why should the 1960s be any different? After talking with his wife, Stan Lee realized that it was his job to make things different. He turned to his longtime collaborator Jack Kirby and together they produced *The Fantastic Four*, the Super Hero comic for people who hated Super Hero comics! *The Fantastic Four* broke every comic-book cliché. They did not wear costumes or have secret identities, were not particularly interested in fighting crime, and squabbled among themselves like a real family. Stan and Jack produced 93 issues and six giant-sized annuals of *The Fantastic Four* during the 1960s. They laid the creative foundation of the entire Marvel Universe, introducing a host of memorable characters, exotic locales, and mind-blowing concepts. Under Stan and Jack, *The Fantastic Four* truly became "The World's Greatest Comic Magazine"!

Fantastic Four Annual #3 (1965). The wedding of Reed Richards and Susan Storm, featuring every Super Hero in the Marvel Universe and every villain the FF had ever fought. (Cover by Jack Kirby)

Strange Tales Annual #2 (1963). The Torch teams up with Spider-Man for the first time.

1961

The Fantastic Four #1 (Nov. 1961). The origin of the FF. (Cover by Jack Kirby)

1962

The Fantastic Four #5 (July 1962). The first appearance of Doom. (Cover by Jack Kirby)

1963

The Fantastic Four #12 (Mar. 1963). The FF meet the Hulk. (Cover by Jack Kirby)

1964

Fantastic Four #26 (May 1964). The FF and the Avengers fight the Hulk. (Cover by Jack Kirby)

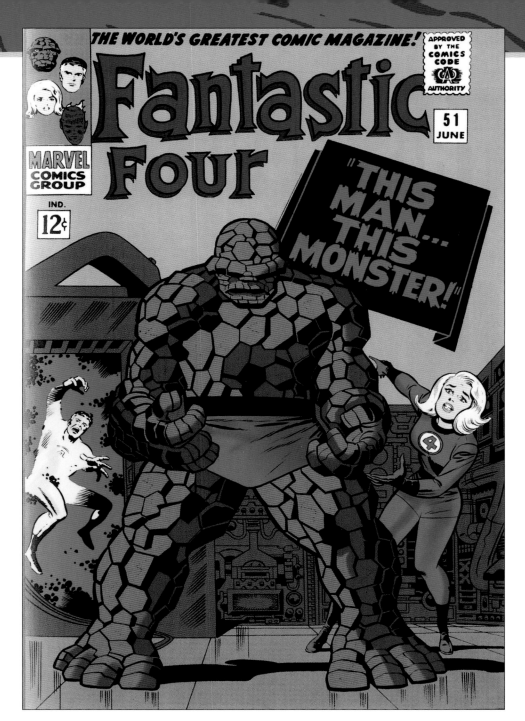

Fantastic Four #28 (July 1964). Tricked by the Mad Thinker and Puppet Master, the uncanny X-Men attack the FF. (Cover by Jack Kirby)

Fantastic Four #51 (June 1966). "This Man, This Monster" explores Ben Grimm's character and is considered to be one of the best FF stories of all time. It also introduces the area of sub-space that will come to be known as the Negative Zone. (Cover by Jack Kirby)

1965

Fantastic Four #36 (Mar. 1965). The FF meet the Frightful Four. (Cover by Jack Kirby)

1966

Fantastic Four #48 (Mar. 1966). The first appearance of Galactus. (Cover by Jack Kirby)

1968

Fantastic Four #78 (Sept. 1968). The Thing regains his humanity. (Cover by Jack Kirby)

1969

Fantastic Four #86 (May 1969). The FF are trapped in Latveria. (Cover by Jack Kirby)

Skrulls

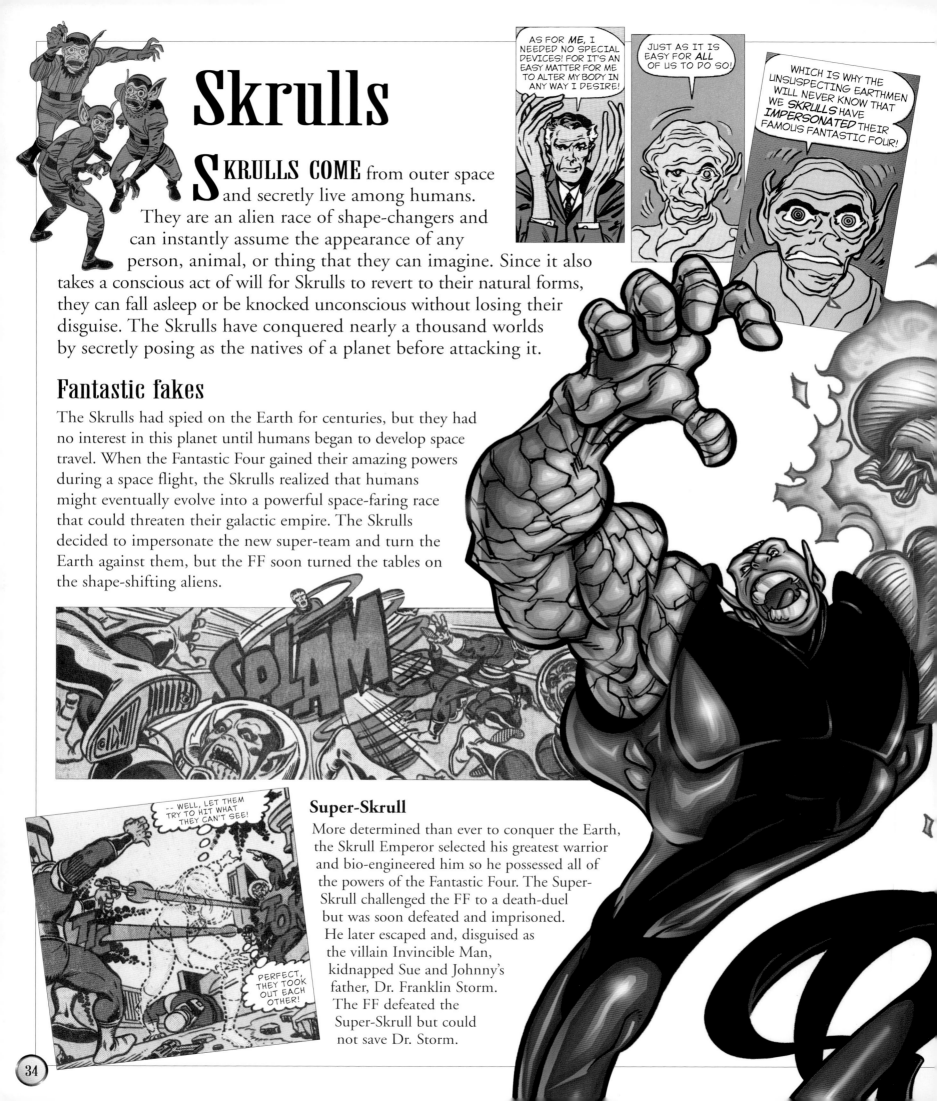

SKRULLS COME from outer space and secretly live among humans. They are an alien race of shape-changers and can instantly assume the appearance of any person, animal, or thing that they can imagine. Since it also takes a conscious act of will for Skrulls to revert to their natural forms, they can fall asleep or be knocked unconscious without losing their disguise. The Skrulls have conquered nearly a thousand worlds by secretly posing as the natives of a planet before attacking it.

AS FOR *ME*, I NEEDED NO SPECIAL DEVICES! FOR IT'S AN EASY MATTER FOR ME TO ALTER MY BODY IN ANY WAY I DESIRE!

JUST AS IT IS EASY FOR *ALL* OF US TO DO SO!

WHICH IS WHY THE UNSUSPECTING EARTHMEN WILL NEVER KNOW THAT WE *SKRULLS* HAVE *IMPERSONATED* THEIR FAMOUS FANTASTIC FOUR!

Fantastic fakes

The Skrulls had spied on the Earth for centuries, but they had no interest in this planet until humans began to develop space travel. When the Fantastic Four gained their amazing powers during a space flight, the Skrulls realized that humans might eventually evolve into a powerful space-faring race that could threaten their galactic empire. The Skrulls decided to impersonate the new super-team and turn the Earth against them, but the FF soon turned the tables on the shape-shifting aliens.

SPLAM

-- WELL, LET THEM TRY TO HIT WHAT THEY CAN'T SEE!

PERFECT, THEY TOOK OUT EACH OTHER!

Super-Skrull

More determined than ever to conquer the Earth, the Skrull Emperor selected his greatest warrior and bio-engineered him so he possessed all of the powers of the Fantastic Four. The Super-Skrull challenged the FF to a death-duel but was soon defeated and imprisoned. He later escaped and, disguised as the villain Invincible Man, kidnapped Sue and Johnny's father, Dr. Franklin Storm. The FF defeated the Super-Skrull but could not save Dr. Storm.

Ravenous empire

There are over 30 billion Skrulls in the universe, and they are all ruled by a single Supreme Emperor or Empress. Their ever-expanding empire extends throughout the Andromeda Galaxy, and it is always encroaching on several neighboring galaxies. The central Skrull government used to be based on a planet called Throneworld, but that was recently consumed by Galactus, the devourer of worlds. The Skrulls are a highly advanced and ruthless race. Their entire economy is built around their military, and they have waged a series of wars for more than a million years with another alien race called the Kree.

THE WARRIOR OF WARRIORS

Though he has never been able to beat the Fantastic Four, the Super-Skrull is an expert in all forms of armed or unarmed combat. Aside from having all the powers of the Fantastic Four, he can also project a hypnotic beam from his eyes that can instantly stun his enemies.

A Skrull takes a slave

Realizing that he could never defeat the Fantastic Four, one enterprising Skrull came up with a new plan. He disguised himself to look like Reed Richards and lured the Thing into a trap. The Skrull kidnapped him and sold him into slavery. The Thing was taken to a distant planet and pitted against a living robot called Torgo in the Arena of Death. Luckily, the FF arrived in time to stop the battle and free all the slaves.

Miracle Man

He was the world's greatest illusionist, a master-hypnotist who could instantly enthrall thousands of people. But the Miracle Man wanted more than mere fame—he desired true power. He used his abilities against the Fantastic Four, wreaking havoc by convincing people that a giant plaster monster was running amok in the city. Miracle Man lost his powers and was defeated when the Torch temporarily blinded him with a burst of flame. He was captured and put in prison, where he studied everything he could about mind control. He learned of a legendary group of Native American shamans who had the power of total mind control, and upon his release, he went in search of them. Under the guidance of the shamans, Miracle Man developed the power to create any reality that he could imagine.

MIND OVER MATTER

With mind control, Miracle Man can become as big and powerful as he wishes.

Sub-Mariner
Prince Namor of Atlantis

Fantastic Four Special Edition *Vol. 1 #1 (May 1984). The Sub-Mariner versus the human race. (Cover art by John Byrne)*

PRINCE NAMOR rules over the undersea Kingdom of Atlantis, home to *Homo Mermanus*—a race of intelligent, water-breathing people. Namor is the son of an Atlantean princess and American sea captain, Leonard McKenzie. His parents met in 1920 when a research vessel, under the command of Captain McKenzie, set off explosive charges in the ocean to break up icebergs. The explosions accidentally sent shockwaves into Atlantis, which was located below. Fearing his kingdom was under attack, the Atlantean Emperor sent his daughter, Princess Fen, to the surface to investigate. She boarded McKenzie's ship and fell in love with the Captain.

Enter the Sub-Mariner

When Princess Fen failed to return, her father assumed that she had been taken prisoner by the surface men and he sent a war party to rescue her. McKenzie fell in the attack, and Fen returned to Atlantis where she gave birth. The heir to the throne was named Namor, meaning "Avenging Son," and grew up with an antagonistic attitude toward surface people. Namor did not trust air-breathers and used his superhuman powers to attack the surface world. He battled the original Human Torch, an android Super Hero who fought crime in the 1940s and 50s, although during World War II, the Sub-Mariner formed an alliance with the Torch and Captain America against the Axis powers. The Sub-Mariner was forgotten until he was rediscovered by Johnny Storm. After arguing with the Thing, Johnny decided to quit the FF and hid in a rundown hotel in New York's Bowery. He discovered an amnesiac derelict who was, in fact, Namor!

IT DON'T MAKE SENSE, CAPTAIN! SHE OUGHT TO BE FROZEN SOLID IN THAT GETUP, BUT SHE AIN'T! AND LOOK AT THE COLOR OF HER SKIN! AND NO ONE CAN SAVVY THAT *LINGO* SHE TALKS!

STRANGE...SHE SEEMS TO BE HAVING DIFFICULTY BREATHING! SHE KEEPS LOOKING AT THE WATER, AS THOUGH SHE WANTS TO RETURN TO IT!

FIRST, WE'VE GOTTA SEE WHAT HE REALLY *LOOKS* LIKE!

SO LET'S GIVE 'IM A LITTLE *SHAVE*!

FLAME ON!

I CAN CONTROL THE FLAME OF MY BODY TO WI'THIN A HAIR'S WIDTH!

WAIT!! HIS FACE NO - -IT - - CAN'T BE!!

IT IS! IT IS!! HE - -HE'S THE *SUB-MARINER!*

Johnny uses his flame to shave and reveal Namor. After his discovery, the Torch flew Namor to the harbor. The ocean water reinvigorated him and restored his memory.

FIRE AND WATER
Namor was far from grateful to Johnny for helping him. When he discovered that Atlantis had been destroyed in his absence, his hostility toward the human race increased. Like the original Torch, Johnny often battled Namor, pitting his fire powers against the sea king.

Sea power

The Sub-Mariner is one of the strongest living creatures on the planet when in the water, but his strength begins to decrease when he is out of the ocean. If Namor were completely cut off from any source of water, he would dehydrate within a week and die. Namor possesses a radar vision that allows him to sense objects in the murky depths of the ocean and he can also communicate telepathically with many forms of undersea life. As well as being able to swim at superhuman speed, Namor has the ability to fly, due to the wings on his ankles.

MUTANT
Namor may be the world's first super-powered mutant. He is a human amphibian, who can easily breathe both in water and air, so he can live on land or in the depths of the ocean.

UNEASY ALLIES
Playing on Namor's hatred toward land-dwellers, Dr. Von Doom occasionally joined forces with the Sub-Mariner. Although Namor helped Doom, he repented when he realized Doom intended to kill Sue Storm along with her FF teammates.

Deadly attractions

During his first battle with the Fantastic Four, Namor fell in love with Sue Storm and offered to spare mankind if she became his bride. To win her, he even bought a movie studio and offered the FF a million dollars to star in a major motion picture when they briefly ran short of funds. Jealous of Reed, the Sub-Mariner once kidnapped Sue and tried to prove his love for her. Though she seemed to be attracted to Namor, Sue eventually decided that Reed was the man for her. Namor later fell in love with and married the Lady Dorma, but she was murdered on their wedding day.

WHY ARE THEY *TAKING* HIM, BORIS?? HE HAS DONE NOTHING! HIS LIFE HAS BEEN SPENT IN HEALING... IN HELPING THE WEAK AND HELPLESS!

BUT HE IS A *GYPSY*, BOY... AS WE *ALL* ARE! IT IS THE PRICE WE MUST PAY!

Doctor Doom
Victor Von Doom

BORN TO peasants in a small village in the tiny Balkan kingdom of Latveria, Victor Von Doom rose to become monarch of his nation and now plots to rule the entire world. His mother, who died when he was still an infant, was considered by many to be a witch. Victor's father, Werner Von Doom, was a gypsy healer, but when he failed to cure a local baron's wife from a terminal disease, he and Victor were forced to flee their village. Werner later died of exposure, and Victor vowed to punish the entire world for the loss of his parents. Using his mother's magical artifacts and book of spells, he began to amass formidable mystical knowledge. His intensive scientific studies also enabled him to build many astounding devices.

IT LOOKS LIKE SOMEONE IS AS ANXIOUS TO SEE THE SCIENCE LAB AS *I* AM! NAME'S RICHARDS, FELLA... REED *RICHARDS*!

THAT IS NO CONCERN OF *MINE*!!

THE LONER
When they first met at University, Reed Richards offered to become Victor Von Doom's roommate, but he had no interest in making friends and snubbed Reed.

Flawed genius

Victor Von Doom's abilities led to the offer of a scholarship at the State University in New York. It was here that he met Reed Richards. When Doom began work on a trans-dimensional projection device, Richards pointed out an error in his calculations. Ignoring the warning, Victor tested the machine. It exploded in his face, leaving a thin scar. Expelled from college, he journeyed to Tibet, where he joined a mysterious order of monks to learn the secrets of sorcery. The monks built him an armored suit and a faceplate to hide his facial flaw, but Doom put on the mask before it had cooled, creating severe, extensive scarring. Renaming himself Doctor Doom, he then returned to Latveria and seized control of the country.

AND NOW... IT IS TIME FOR... *THE MASK!!*

BUT, MASTER, IT HAS NOT COMPLETELY *COOLED* YET!

SAY NO MORE, MY BROTHER! HE WILL TOLERATE NO FURTHER DELAY! SUCH A MAN CANNOT WAIT, AS OTHERS CAN!

NEVER AGAIN WILL MORTAL EYES GAZE UPON THE HIDEOUS COUNTENANCE OF VICTOR VON DOOM!

...WISER...STRONGER! MORE BRILLIANT, MORE POWERFUL THAN EVER BEFORE!!

FROM THIS MOMENT ON, I SHALL BE KNOWN AS... *DOCTOR DOOM!*

ORIGIN OF DOOM
Donning fearsome armor and a mask to hide his scarred face, Victor becomes Doctor Doom.

AH!! MY THREE EMISSARIES! YOU HAVE RETURNED! AS I *KNEW* YOU WOULD!

REED! NOT THE *ENCEPHALO - GUN!!* NOT *THAT!!* YOU *CAN'T!!*

STAND BACK, SUE! IT'S THE *ONLY* WAY! IF I SHOULD *LOSE*, MY DARLING, REMEMBER... I'VE LOVED YOU FROM THE FIRST!! NOTHING CAN EVER CHANGE THAT!

FINE WORDS, RICHARDS!..FROM ONE ABOUT TO *DIE!!* WITH THIS DEVICE SET AT *FULL POWER*, THE ONE WITH THE GREATER MENTALITY WILL SEND THE OTHER TO A TIME-LESS LIMBO FROM WHICH THERE IS NO RETURN! AND NOW... *BEGIN!!*

Bitter rivals

Doom's desire for conquest eventually led to conflict with Reed Richards, now the leader of the Fantastic Four. Doom forced the FF to go back in time to search for the magic gems of Merlin, which would make him invincible. Defeated, he unsuccessfully tried to strand the FF, firstly in outer space and then in a micro-universe. Obsessed with trying to prove his superiority over Reed, Doom challenged him to a deadly battle of minds using the Encephalo-Gun. Reed's sudden disappearance led Doom to believe he had won. However, he had been duped, once again outwitted by his old adversary.

A formidable foe

Doctor Doom's mastery of science extends into the fields of robotics, weapons technology, and biochemistry. His nuclear-powered, computer-enhanced body armor is equipped with various offensive and defensive weapons, including gauntlet particle-beam blasters, force fields, and the ability to charge the armor's surface with 30,000 volts of electricity. A compact jet pack enables him to fly. Doom is a master of hand-to-hand combat, and through his study of the mystic arts, he has learned how to transfer his mind into other bodies. As the ruler of Latveria, he also has full diplomatic immunity and cannot be arrested in the U.S.A.

A Doombot blasts the FF with its eye-slit energy rays.

USEFUL DEVICES

Doctor Doom's technical skills have enabled him to create many handy gadgets, such as the hypnotism impulser (left) and the gravity sensitizer (below).

SUCH AS MY *INSTANT HYPNOTISM* IMPULSER, WHICH CAN UPSET YOUR TOTAL SENSE OF BALANCE IN ONE SPLIT-SECOND!

HUH? HEY-- EVERYTHING'S SPINNIN' AROUND! CAN'T STAY ON MY FEET! MY LEGS ARE GETTIN' WOBBLY! WHAT'S GOIN' ON??!

YOU ARE BATTLING NO *NORMAL* FOE NOW, UGLY ONE! IN MY SPECIAL ARMOR -- WITH MY SPECIAL WEAPONS -- I'M FAR MORE POWERFUL THAN *YOU*!

THIS MINIATURIZED *SENSITIZER* WHICH I PLACE UPON YOUR BACK USES NUCLEAR ENERGY TO INCREASE THE FORCE OF *GRAVITY*!

YOU *CREEP*! IT'LL TAKE MORE THAN *THAT* TO STOP *ME*!

WE ARE EVEN PROGRAMMED TO *BELIEVE OURSELVES* TO BE THE TRUE DOOM, SAVE WHEN IN THE PRESENCE OF THE MASTER OR ONE OF OUR ROBOT BROTHERS.

BUT EVEN WITH THAT THE MASTER DID NOT WISH *US* TO HOLD CONTROL OVER THE PEOPLES OF LATVERIA FOREVER. FOR THAT PURPOSE HE SELECTED A *HUMAN* HEIR. *YOU.*

Kristoff Vernard

After the failure of his attempt to create an heir through cloning experiments, Doom took the orphaned child Kristoff Vernard under his care when the boy's mother was accidentally killed by Latverian rebels. Doom made Kristoff his heir, schooling him to rule Latveria with a firm hand. Doom's robotic replicas, the Doombots, usually ruled Latveria in his absence, but when it appeared that Doom had died at the hands of Terrax, they programmed Kristoff's mind with all of Doom's memories. Believing that he was actually Victor Von Doom, Kristoff launched an attack on the Fantastic Four. This continued until the real Doom returned to claim his throne, restoring Kristoff's own identity using a memory switch implanted in his brain.

NO, I'M DOOM...I'M THE *ONLY*... THE ONLY... I...I...

I...FEEL LIKE I'M WAKING UP, SIRE, IS THAT *YOU*? HAVE YOU SAVED ME FROM A NIGHTMARE? WHAT WAS IT YOU *SAID*?

Kristoff Vernard, believing himself to be Doctor Doom, prepares to don the Super Villain's mask.

Puppet Master

PHILIP MASTERS was born in the Balkans and moved to the United States when he was eight years old. A shy and lonely child, he spent most of his time carving wooden marionettes and sculpting figures out of clay. He studied biology in college and became partners with his friend Jacob Reiss in a small research firm. Their company studied a special radioactive clay that Masters had discovered in his homeland. Reiss was married and had a young daughter named Alicia. Over time Masters became insanely jealous of his partner and decided to steal the clay for himself. He planted a bomb in the building to destroy the business, but it accidentally killed Reiss and blinded his daughter. Overcome with guilt, Philip Masters married his partner's widow and adopted Alicia.

From Masters to Master

Masters discovered that his radioactive clay had a special power. If he made a lifelike puppet of someone, he could mentally force that person to do his bidding. To test his power, the Puppet Master commanded one of his victims to commit suicide by leaping off a bridge, but the Human Torch rescued the man. Furious at the FF's interference, Masters promptly carved a puppet of the Thing and turned him against his teammates. Mr. Fantastic freed the Thing by temporarily changing him back into his human form, and the team then managed to defeat the Puppet Master.

The Puppet Master can only control one person at a time, and his power begins to weaken as his subject moves farther away from him.

Pawns of the Puppet Master

The Puppet Master believed that it was his destiny to rule the entire planet. He intended to force all the government leaders into merging their lands into a single kingdom that he would control. Since the Fantastic Four stood in his way, he constantly tried to destroy them. He once pitted the Human Torch against the Thing and later attacked them both with life-sized action figures. He also compelled the Sub-Mariner to kidnap the Invisible Girl.

THEN, AFTER THE CLAY HAS BEEN TREATED AND COATED WITH A THIN FILM OF LEAD PAINT...

MY REVENGE WILL BE MUCH SWEETER IF I DO NOT MANIPULATE THE FANTASTIC FOUR! INSTEAD, I SHALL LEAVE THEM THEIR FREE WILL, WHILE THE SUB-MARINER, UNDER MY CONTROL, DEFEATS THEM!

The Puppet Master planned to make the FF his personal slaves when he became the king of the world.

THERE! IT IS DONE!

FASHIONING A UNIFORM LIKE HERS AND A BLONDE WIG FOR YOU ARE CHILD'S PLAY FOR THE PUPPET MASTER!

ALL FOR ALICIA

Though he once disguised his stepdaughter as Sue Storm and used her to trick the Fantastic Four, the Puppet Master truly loves Alicia and has often put her happiness above his own.

AND NOW, ALICIA, WHILE OUR UNINVITED GUEST SLEEPS, YOU WILL TAKE HER PLACE! YOU WILL PLAY A HARMLESS LITTLE PRANK FOR ME!

A LITTLE PRANK? BUT WHAT, FATHER?

YOU WERE ABLE TO STEAL THAT MIGHTY ANDROID FROM MR. FANTASTIC?? THEN - -YOU MUST BE EVEN MORE BRILLIANT THAN I HEARD YOU WERE!

OF COURSE! THAT IS WHY MY PLAN TO CONQUER THE FANTASTIC FOUR CANNOT FAIL - - AND THAT IS WHY YOU WILL HELP ME!

Partners in crime

After being defeated many times, the Puppet Master gave up and went into hiding. But the Mad Thinker found him and convinced him that they should join forces. Together, they plotted the Fantastic Four's downfall, tricking the X-Men into fighting them and also attacking the FF with an army of androids who resembled all their past enemies.

"ON POPPUP, OUR EVOLUTIONARY PROCESSES ARE SO SWIFT, THAT WE CAN CHANGE OURSELVES INTO ANYTHING, IN ORDER TO SURVIVE THE MENACES WHICH CONSTANTLY ATTACK US!"

THAT URRPO-FISH WILL BREAK HIS TEETH IF HE TRIES TO BITE ME NOW!

POP!

Impossible Man

The Impossible Man was born on a distant planet called Poppup, a world filled with dangerous monsters. The inhabitants had to evolve quickly in order to survive and so they developed into a race of shape-changers. The Impossible Man was bored with life on Poppup and turned himself into a spaceship so he could explore the universe. He eventually landed on Earth, where he met the Fantastic Four and made a nuisance of himself with his ridiculous transformations. Poppup was later destroyed by Galactus, and the Impossible Man became the last of his race until he decided to clone himself and form an Impossible Woman. The happy couple later cloned an entire Impossible Family, and they are presently touring the universe together.

NAME? WE POPPUPIANS HAVE NO NAMES! WE KNOW WHO WE ARE! AND NOW, GOOD DAY!

WE, CAN'T JUST LET HIM WALK AWAY! HE HAS TOO MUCH POWER TO BE LOOSE ON EARTH!

WELL, WHAT DO WE DO NOW?

LET'S ALL RUSH 'IM AT ONCE!

The Hulk

DON'T MAKE him angry—you won't like him when he's angry! After being caught in the heart of a nuclear explosion and bathed in Gamma radiation, Dr. Robert Bruce Banner now finds himself transformed into the incredible Hulk during times of stress. The Hulk is one of the most powerful creatures to ever walk the Earth, and his strength grows in direct proportion to his anger. Over the years, the Hulk has been both a hero and villain, possessing the intelligence of Banner on some occasions and being a mindless monster on others.

AND THEN, ONE OF THE MOST DRAMATIC MOMENTS IN THE HISTORY OF ADVENTURE-FANTASY OCCURS, AS THE INCREDIBLE *HULK* SUDDENLY HURLS HIMSELF INTO THE OPEN, FACE-TO-FACE WITH THE MIGHTY *THING!*

I'LL CRUSH YOU LIKE A FLEA!

IT'S *HIM!* THE *HULK!*

Mission: stop the Hulk!

The Fantastic Four first encountered the Hulk when General Thaddeus E. Ross requested their aid. Ross's missile base was being sabotaged, and he suspected the Hulk. The FF traveled to New Mexico, where they fought the Hulk before discovering that a foreign spy had actually caused the damage. They fought the Hulk again when he came to New York City to destroy the Avengers.

THESE ARE THE MOST RECENT RECORDED MOVING PICTURES OF THE *HULK* HIMSELF! THEY WERE TAKEN BY AN AUTOMATIC CAMERA PLACED IN THE SIGHTING DEVICE OF A SPECIAL CANNON!

WELL, I GUESS WE'RE LOOKING AT PROOF POSITIVE THAT HE *DOES* EXIST!

OUTMATCHED

The Thing is not as big, strong, or ruthless as the Hulk, but he is much too stubborn to back down from a fight.

Battling buddies
The Thing and the Hulk have fought each other many times. Ben was once temporarily driven mad, and thHulk stopped the Thing from going on a rampage.

UNSTOPPABLE

The Hulk's skin is strong enough to withstand direct hits by hand grenades and artillery shells—as well as the high-impact blows of the Thing! When he slams his fists together, the Hulk creates shock waves so powerful that his enemies are sent flying. He can also cause minor earthquakes just by pounding his fists on the ground.

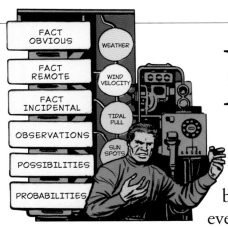

Mad Thinker

LITTLE IS known about the man who calls himself the Thinker but is called the Mad Thinker by everyone else. He was a successful criminal mastermind for years yet the police did not even know he existed. Using a vast network of computers he could predict a likely sequence of events down to the smallest detail, and this enabled him to plot intricate crimes that were virtually foolproof. He outsmarted the law at every turn until he came up against the Fantastic Four.

Kingdom of crime

The Thinker devised a plan to seize control of New York City and turn it into an independent nation. He would rule this new nation, and the country's major crime bosses would serve as both his enforcers and his ambassadors to the other American cities. Only the Fantastic Four stood in his way so he arranged for the team to leave New York. In their absence, the Thinker took over the Baxter Building, but the FF returned unexpectedly and defeated him.

HEY! NOW WHAT'S HAPPENIN' ??

I WAS AFRAID OF THAT BEN! THE ANDROID HAS THE POWER OF MIMICRY BUILT INTO IT-- IT'S TURNING INTO --YOU!

Awesome android

Whilst in the Baxter Building, the Thinker used some of Reed's research to construct an artificial creature, 15 feet tall. Made of robotic and organic parts, the android was super-strong and could mimic the physical properties of anything it touched.

VIRTUAL FREEDOM
The Thinker developed a way of projecting his mind into an android body so he could continue his criminal activities from a prison cell.

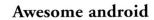
QUASIMODO

QUASIMODO
Originally designed to be the Thinker's ultimate computer, Quasimodo is a robot who was given a humanlike form by the Silver Surfer. He possesses super-strength and his left eye can project bursts of concussive force.

S'LONG, HORNHEAD, IT'S A CRYIN' SHAME YOU HADDA GET MIXED UP IN THIS.

THEN YOUR DECISION IS MADE, DAREDEVIL. VERY WELL, I WILL CONSOLE MYSELF WITH THE DEATH OF A MEMBER OF THE FANTASTIC FOUR!

BLAST! THERE MUST BE SOMETHING I CAN DO! IF ONLY THE THINK-ER WASN'T CONVINCED I'M SOME SORT OF PSYCHIC!

WAIT! MAYBE THAT'S IT!

ALL RIGHT, THINKER, I CONFESS. I AM ABLE TO FORESEE THE FUTURE--AND CHANGE IT IF MY FORESIGHT IS ACTED UPON IN TIME.

Obsessed with finding a way to defeat the FF, the Thinker once became convinced that Daredevil could predict the future. The Thinker threatened to kill the Thing in order to assure Daredevil's cooperation.

SET THE CONTROLS, COMRADE GORILLA!

YOU OTHERS SETTLE BACK IN YOUR SAFETY SEATS! OUR GREAT MOMENT IS AT HAND!

The Red Ghost Ivan Kragoff

IVAN **K**RAGOFF was a Russian scientist who worked for the former Soviet Union. He became fascinated by the Fantastic Four and began to study their history. Kragoff believed he could recreate the accident that gave the FF their super-powers, and he convinced his government to build a spaceship that was specifically designed to expose its crew to cosmic rays. Instead of testing his theory on other humans, Kragoff decided to use two great apes and a monkey that he trained for the mission. Blasting into space on the same day that the Fantastic Four had embarked on their journey, Kragoff and his apes headed directly into a cosmic storm that transformed them into the infamous Red Ghost and his fiendish Super-Apes.

Untouchable

After being exposed to the cosmic rays, Kragoff gained the ability to become a living phantom. He can become intangible at will and is able to make part of his body solid while the rest remains insubstantial. Although he cannot turn invisible, he can make his body transparent. He has acquired the ability to assume a mistlike form so that he looks like a real ghost.

AND NOW IT *BEGINS!* WE ARE PASSING THRU THE COSMIC BELT! I CAN *FEEL* THE RAYS! THEY SHALL GIVE ME POWER! *POWER! POWER!*

THEN, I CAN *SNAP* THEM FORWARD LIKE A PAPERCLIP IN A *RUBBER BAND*...

THERE! IT WORKED. I'VE BACK MY FULL *RESILIENCY!*

IN FACT, I MAY EVEN BE MORE *POWERFUL* THAN BEFORE!

Kragoff's powers make him a formidable opponent—even for Mr. Fantastic. Bullets and missiles pass right through him and no prison can hold him for long.

QUITE GOOD, RICHARDS. EXCELLENT, IN FACT.

EXCEPT YOU'VE FORGOTTEN *MY* INCREDIBLE POWERS.

HOW CAN YOU HARM AN *INTANGIBLE* MAN?

BAKAMM

Evenly matched?

Kragoff keeps trying to prove that he is Mr. Fantastic's physical and intellectual superior, but the Red Ghost has lost every battle they have ever fought.

LOOK OUT, BEN! I WARNED YOU! HE CAN *TRANSFORM* HIMSELF!!

STOP STRUGGLIN' SMALL FRY! YOU'VE GOT AS MUCH CHANCE OF BREAKIN' MY GRIP AS YOU GOT OF WINNIN' THE *MISS AMERICA* CONTEST!

HEY! WHAT'S *GOIN' ON* HERE??

YEEEOWW! HE TURNED HIMSELF INTO A BLASTED BALL OF IRON *SPIKES!!*

MIGHTY APES

Igor the baboon acquired the ability to transform his body into any object, animal, or shape that he could imagine. He could become a living ball of spikes or resemble a machine gun. Peator the orangutan obtained magneticlike powers and can repel or attract any object that contains even the slightest trace of metal.

Simian assistants

Kragoff owned and trained the three anthropoids that became his Super-Apes. Mikhlo the gorilla gained so much super-strength that he was even stronger than the Thing, and his strength has continued to increase over time.

OLD ENEMIES

The Red Ghost has often fought the Fantastic Four over the years. He once kidnapped the FF and forced them to return to the Moon for a rematch of their first battle. He also tried to steal the Watcher's alien technology and joined the army of Super Villains who attacked Reed and Sue on their wedding day.

STEP ABOARD, ALL OF YOU! WE ARE ABOUT TO BEGIN OUR JOURNEY... A JOURNEY FROM WHICH YOU SHALL NEVER RETURN!

Trading places

The Red Ghost and his Super-Apes recently attempted to unleash 1,000 gallons of toxic nerve gas on the people of New York. As he battled his old foes, Reed Richards realized that the personalities and super-powers of Kragoff and his simians had started to merge. The Super-Apes had gained the ability to think and speak, while Kragoff seemed to have lost his intelligence.

I RECOGNIZE YOU! YOU -- YOU'RE *DR. IVAN KRAGOFF,* THE *RUSSIAN COSMONAUT* WHO FLEW INTO SPACE --

-- AND *DELIBERATELY EXPOSED* HIMSELF TO *COSMIC RAYS!*

AND THESE MUST BE YOUR... *HENCHMEN?!*

MUCH *MORE* THAN THAT, CHILD --

-- WE ARE *THE SUPER APES!*

MIKHLO...

...PEATOR...

...AND IGOR, *RESPECTIVELY.*

OUR INTENT, DR. POLOMBO, WAS TO KEEP OUR PRESENCE A *SECRET* UNTIL THE *ABSOLUTE LAST MOMENT* BEFORE THE *CONTAMINATION...*

...BUT YOUR RATHER *SLAVISH DEDICATION* TO YOUR STUDIES HAS *FORCED* OUR PAWS, AS IT WERE.

CONTAMINATION?

IN A MANNER OF SPEAKING BEN...YES.

IS IT ME, OR IS IVAN A BIT *"LESS SMART"* THAN HE *USED TO BE?*

IVAN *KEEP* BUNNY?

IVAN *LOVE* BUNNY!

THAT IS *ONE WAY* OF PUTTING IT. I SUSPECT THAT KRAGOFF'S *DIMINISHED* INTELLECT IS ALSO THE RESULT OF HIS SUPER-APES' MACHINATIONS.

AS YOU KNOW, WE WATCHERS ARE FORBIDDEN TO INTERFERE WITH PEOPLE OF OTHER PLANETS! BUT, SO GRAVE IS THIS *DANGER,* THAT IT MIGHT EVEN DESTROY MY *OWN* RACE!

FOR, AS LONG AS THIS CREATURE EXISTS, THE ENTIRE *UNIVERSE* IS IN PERIL!

WHO, OR WHAT *IS* THIS DANGER? HOW CAN *ANY-THING* THREATEN THIS ENTIRE *UNIVERSE?*

The Watcher

His name is Uatu the all-seeing Watcher. Uatu belongs to an incredibly powerful alien race that secretly observes everything that happens in the universe. Assigned to watch the Earth, Uatu lives in the Blue Area of the Moon. The Watcher is virtually immortal and possesses immeasurable psionic abilities. He can also convert his body into pure energy and instantly transport himself anywhere in the universe. Uatu met the FF on their first visit to the Moon and instantly developed a fondness for them. Though he is forbidden to interfere in the affairs of other races, the Watcher has often helped the Fantastic Four to save the Earth from various super-menaces.

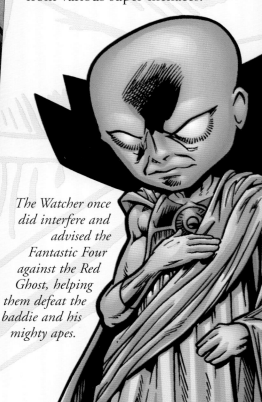

The Watcher once did interfere and advised the Fantastic Four against the Red Ghost, helping them defeat the baddie and his mighty apes.

Rama-Tut
aka Kang, Immortus, & Scarlet Centurion

WHA... WHAT *HAPPENED* TO US?? WHERE *ARE* WE?

WE'VE BEEN BROUGHT TO A THRONE ROOM! WE'RE PRISONERS OF...THE *PHARAOH!*

ON YOUR *FEET*, CAPTIVES! YOU ARE IN THE PRESENCE OF THE AWESOME *RAMA-TUT*, KING OF KINGS, MASTER OF MEN, LORD OF THE SEVEN SUNS!

RAMA-TUT CAME from the year 3000, a glorious age of peace and progress—and he was bored out of his mind! Instead of posterity and enlightenment, he craved action and adventure. After accidentally discovering that one of his ancestors had built a time machine, he spent years trying to recreate it. He built his time machine to look like the Sphinx and journeyed to ancient Egypt where he used his scientific knowledge to become the absolute monarch of the ancient world.

"THEN, ONE DAY, WHILE VISITING THE RUINS OF AN AMAZING ANCESTOR OF MINE, I CAME UPON WHAT WAS LEFT OF HIS GREATEST INVENTION...A *TIME MACHINE!*

PART OF THE MACHINE STILL REMAINS...AND HERE ARE THE PLANS FOR ITS OPERATION!

IT WOULD BE SIMPLE FOR ME TO RECREATE IT AND USE IT FOR MY OWN PURPOSES!

Prisoners of the pharaoh

While investigating hieroglyphics at a natural history museum, Mr. Fantastic became convinced that the ancient Egyptians had a cure for blindness. Hoping to cure Alicia Masters, he gathered the rest of the Fantastic Four and used their time machine to travel into the past. With the aid of his futuristic weaponry, Rama-Tut captured the FF, but they escaped and forced the pharaoh to flee back to the future.

Time traumas

As Rama-Tut journeyed back to the year 3000, he encountered a disruption in the time stream that caused him to create a number of alternate realities. In one reality, he landed on a version of present-day Earth and convinced the Avengers to take control of the Earth. In another, he found himself on a war-torn Earth in the year 4000 and ultimately conquered it.

Related to Reed

Rama-Tut first believed that he was a descendant of Doctor Doom, but his ancient ancestor was actually Nathaniel Richards, the father of Reed Richards. After Reed's mother died, Nathaniel journeyed to an alternate Earth, remarried, and had another son, whose bloodline eventually produced Rama-Tut.

"FINALLY, I PLANNED TO RETURN TO MY *OWN* CENTURY, THE YEAR 3,000! SO, I ADJUSTED THE MOLECULAR TIME-DRIVE TO THE PROPER SETTING...

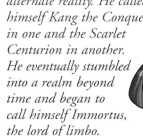

Rama-Tut adopted a different identity in each alternate reality. He called himself Kang the Conqueror in one and the Scarlet Centurion in another. He eventually stumbled into a realm beyond time and began to call himself Immortus, the lord of limbo.

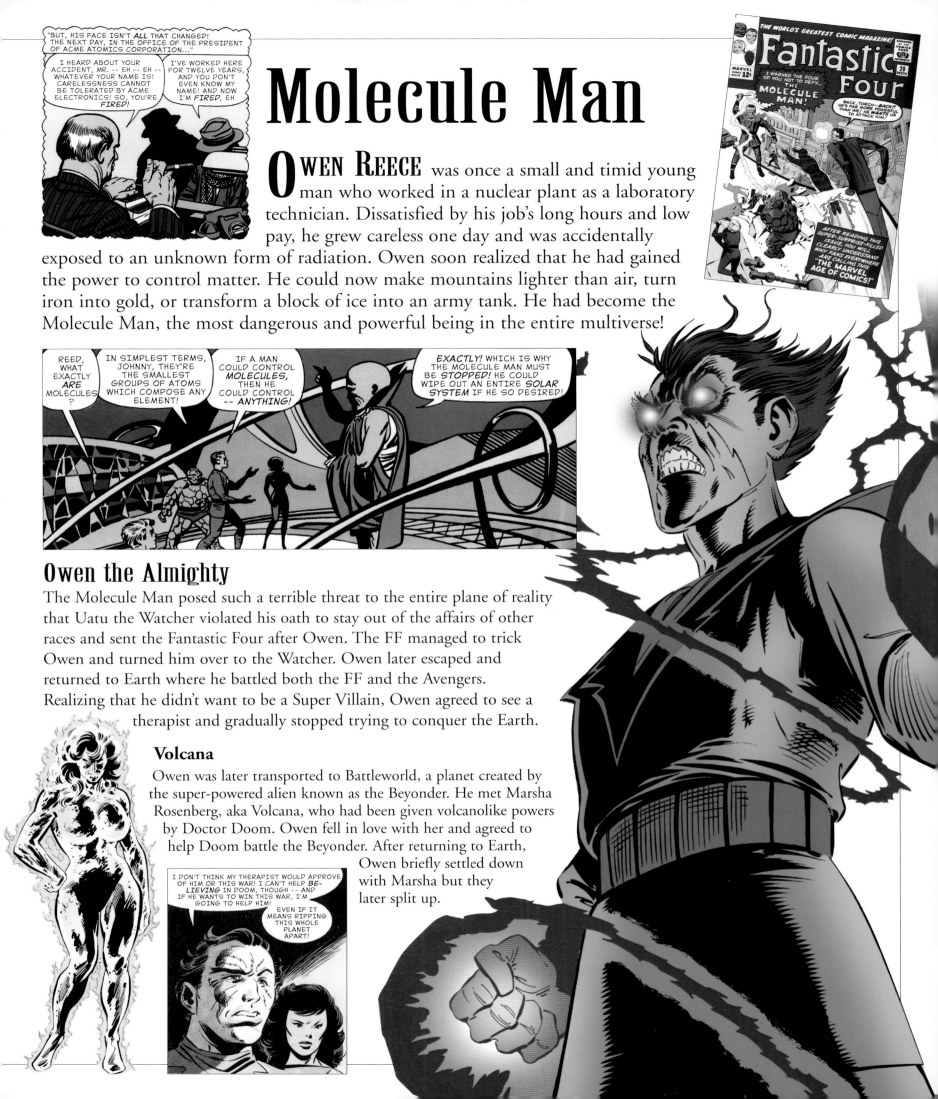

Molecule Man

OWEN REECE was once a small and timid young man who worked in a nuclear plant as a laboratory technician. Dissatisfied by his job's long hours and low pay, he grew careless one day and was accidentally exposed to an unknown form of radiation. Owen soon realized that he had gained the power to control matter. He could now make mountains lighter than air, turn iron into gold, or transform a block of ice into an army tank. He had become the Molecule Man, the most dangerous and powerful being in the entire multiverse!

Owen the Almighty

The Molecule Man posed such a terrible threat to the entire plane of reality that Uatu the Watcher violated his oath to stay out of the affairs of other races and sent the Fantastic Four after Owen. The FF managed to trick Owen and turned him over to the Watcher. Owen later escaped and returned to Earth where he battled both the FF and the Avengers. Realizing that he didn't want to be a Super Villain, Owen agreed to see a therapist and gradually stopped trying to conquer the Earth.

Volcana

Owen was later transported to Battleworld, a planet created by the super-powered alien known as the Beyonder. He met Marsha Rosenberg, aka Volcana, who had been given volcanolike powers by Doctor Doom. Owen fell in love with her and agreed to help Doom battle the Beyonder. After returning to Earth, Owen briefly settled down with Marsha but they later split up.

THE MOST *POTENT* AND *POWERFUL* OF MY ALCHEMIST'S ART!

THE TIME FOR *SUBTLETY* IS PAST. IF THERE IS HOPE FOR *VICTORY*, IT LIES IN DESTROYING ALL WHO OPPOSE ME.

--DESTROYING-- THEM *NOW!*

Diablo

DIABLO IS the world's greatest master of the ancient science of alchemy, an early form of chemistry that sought to transform base metals into gold. Born to a rich Spanish nobleman in the early ninth century, Esteban Diablo believed that he could use alchemy to rule humanity, and he traveled the world to study it. He hunted down powerful artifacts, amassed secret formulas, experimented with bizarre potions, and searched for rare herbs. As his mastery of the arcane art grew, so did his personal power. Diablo discovered an elixir that could slow aging to the point that he became temporarily immortal. He later acquired a castle in Transylvania, where he set up a laboratory and terrorized the local countryside for centuries. The villagers revolted and imprisoned him within a massive crypt. Diablo was trapped for more than 100 years, dreaming of his revenge.

Potion power

Diablo possesses an enormous collection of potions that seem almost magical in nature. His concoctions include pellets full of nerve gas, medicines that cause people to experience wild hallucinations, a potion that instantly lowers a person's body temperature to freeze them in place, and one that makes a person susceptible to Diablo's will. His costume is lined with hidden pockets and pouches, where he keeps his various elixirs and alchemical weapons.

Free at last

While on a vacation to Transylvania, the Fantastic Four stumbled upon the abandoned castle of Diablo. A local Baron warned them to stay away from it and told them of the terrible legends surrounding Diablo. One night, the Thing heard a whisper and followed the voice to a hidden crypt. Ben used his strength to smash the stone slab that held the alchemist prisoner, and Diablo was set loose. Determined to become master of all mankind, Diablo wanted to secure the help of the Thing.

DIABOLIC ALCHEMY

Diablo has allegedly transformed stones into feathers and caused simple seeds to grow instantly into vast jungles. He changes his appearance by manipulating the flesh on his face and can make his body invulnerable to harm. He can also control inorganic matter and the bodies of others.

ALLOW ME TO PRESENT MYSELF! I AM KNOWN AS -- DIABLO!! AND THIS IS MY NEW ASSISTANT-- THE ONE YOU USED TO CALL THE THING!

HE'S GOT YOU BEAT A MILE, REEDY BOY! LOOK HOW GORGEOUS HE MADE ME-- WITH JUST ONE SIP OF A POTION OF HIS!

WE'RE DELIGHTED FOR YOU, BEN-- BUT WHAT DID HE MEAN BY REFERRING TO YOU AS HIS ASSISTANT??

The pawn and the potion

The rest of the Fantastic Four learned of Ben's absence the next morning and followed his trail to the castle. They discovered that Diablo had mixed a potion that improved Ben's appearance. Believing that the alchemist could restore Ben's humanity so that he could marry Alicia Masters, Ben agreed to serve Diablo for one year. Diablo sold his potions and used the money to build an army to conquer the world. When the potions wore off, Ben regained his senses and chased Diablo into his crypt.

HOW ABOUT THAT, PAL??! THAT'S WHAT HE DID TO ME--TURNED ME INTO A BLUSHIN' ROSE!

HE'S DONE MORE THAN THAT! HE'S MANAGED TO INFLUENCE YOU -- TO STEAL YOUR LOYALTY! BUT HE WON'T GET AWAY WITH IT...!

While Diablo's elixirs can accomplish some amazing feats, Reed Richards discovered that the effects are only temporary.

HOLD IT, STRINGBEAN! MAYBE YOU DIDN'T DIG ME BEFORE! I'M WORKIN' FOR DIABLO NOW! NOBODY TACKLES HIM WHILE I'M AROUND! NOT EVEN YOU!

DO NOT FORGET, MY IMPETUOUS INTRUDERS--THE THING IS NOW IN MY DEBT! ONLY I HAVE BEEN ABLE TO IMPROVE HIS APPEARANCE--PERMANENTLY!

Back to basics

Diablo has returned on numerous occasions. He once battled Doctor Doom and was exiled into an alternate dimension. After gaining freedom, Diablo kidnapped Crystal and attempted to stir up a revolution in a small Central American country so that he could exploit the country's natural resources for his alchemy. He also created elemental beings composed of earth, fire, air, and water and repeatedly sent them to destroy the Fantastic Four. Though recently reportedly killed in a battle with Alpha Flight, a team of Canadian Super Heroes, Diablo has successfully cheated death for more than 1,000 years.

-- MY DRAGON MAN!! IT COMBINES THE GREATEST POWERS I COULD GIVEN AN ARTIFICIA... CREATION A MIGHTY TAIL BUILT-IN HEAT REACTORS WHICH EMIT FLAME AT THE TOUCH OF A BUTTON -- WINGS WHICH --

ENOUGH! SPARE ME THE DETAILS! ONE LOOK IS ALL I NEED! HE SHALL SERVE MY PURPOSES ADMIRABLY!

NOW, YOU MUST OBEY ME IMPLICITLY, AND I SHALL SHOW YOU WONDERS BEYOND YOUR WILDEST DREAMS!!

Dragon Man

Professor Gregson Gilbert was a biologist specializing in super-powered humans. He attempted to construct a robot more powerful than anything that lived. Dragon Man was the result. However, it was redundant until Diablo used alchemy to give the creature artificial life. Dragon Man stands over 15 feet high and weighs more than 3 tons. It can fly, has super-strength, and can exhale fire like a real dragon. Its 7-foot-long tail can move nearly 90 miles an hour and is strong enough to shatter a stone wall. Possessing the intelligence of the average dog, Dragon Man is usually used as a pawn by other villains. The creature has formed a special attachment to Sue Richards and has often tried to capture her.

STOP HIM! HE'S GOT MY WIFE-- MY CHILD!

BUT---IF WE MAKE HIM LET GO OF THEM--

--THEY'LL FALL TO THEIR DEATHS!!

A GATHERING OF EVIL

Sandman and Trapster waited eagerly to meet the fourth member of their new team. When the Wizard introduced them to Medusa, they were impressed. Now, with their combined powers, the Fantastic Four could finally be defeated.

Frightful Four

TWO CRIMINALS, Paste Pot Pete (later known as Trapster) and Sandman, escaped from prison and met the Wizard, a villain who had just suffered yet another defeat at the hands of the Torch. They realized that they stood a much better chance of defeating their common enemy—the Fantastic Four—if they joined forces. All they needed was one more member to be the FF's evil counterpart. The Wizard heard of a mysterious woman known as Madam Medusa who possessed extraordinary powers and knew he had found the perfect addition to their team. Once Madam Medusa was in place, the Frightful Four were ready to embark on a crusade of crime.

The evil FF

The Frightful Four planned their first attack on the Fantastic Four to coincide with a party held at the Baxter Building to celebrate the engagement of Sue and Reed. They waited until all the Super Hero guests had left before storming the FF headquarters. They managed to capture Reed, Sue, Ben, and Alicia Masters, but luckily Johnny had already left to meet friends. The Wizard put his captives to sleep, tied them together, and attached a powerful anti-gravity disc to each of them before setting them adrift from the roof of the Baxter Building. The Frightful Four congratulated each other on their success as they watched their enemies float higher and higher and were furious when the Torch arrived to save his friends and thwart their evil plans.

THE WIZARD

The Wizard was a celebrity, known throughout the world for inventing futuristic devices that he sold to the rich. He became jealous of the publicity the Fantastic Four were receiving—the Torch in particular—so he invented a costume that allowed him to master the force of gravity and mimic the Torch's powers.

TRAPSTER

Peter Petruski was a research chemist who invented a super-strong paste and decided to use it to embark on a career of crime. Calling himself Paste Pot Pete, he developed numerous weapons that dispensed his paste with pin-point accuracy, trapping victims instantly and rendering them helpless for hours. He later changed his name to the Trapster.

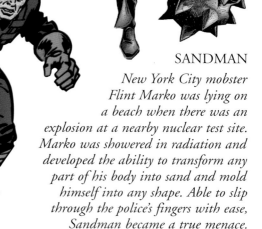

SANDMAN

New York City mobster Flint Marko was lying on a beach when there was an explosion at a nearby nuclear test site. Marko was showered in radiation and developed the ability to transform any part of his body into sand and mold himself into any shape. Able to slip through the police's fingers with ease, Sandman became a true menace.

53 of 148

INHUMAN ALLY

Suffering from amnesia, an Inhuman named Medusa wandered the Mediterranean, committing small crimes to survive. The Wizard heard rumors of the woman with living hair and discovered her in a cave on the French coast. He rescued her and took her to the United States. Since she was grateful for his help, Medusa agreed to join the Frightful Four.

The legion of substitute villains

Eventually Medusa's memory returned and she left the Frightful Four. She was replaced by a villain named Thundra, but she quit soon after. The remaining members of the Frightful Four captured the Fantastic Four, assumed control of the Baxter Building, and held auditions for a fourth member. They chose the man-monster known as the Brute. The Wizard also convinced Electro, the master of electricity, to briefly join the team and even tried to trick Spider-Man into attacking the FF. Disgusted with his former partners, the Wizard formed an all-new Frightful Four that consisted of Klaw, Hydro-Man, who can transform his body into water, and Titania, a woman with superhuman strength.

Salamandra the Fire Maiden can transform herself into a fierce fire-breathing dragon.

Dysfunctional

The Wizard recently reformed the Frightful Four. He brought back the Trapster and Hydro-Man and added his ex-wife Salamandra the Fire Maiden. She has the ability to project blue flames and can transform herself into a dragonlike creature. The Wizard also attempted to include his daughter Cole, who can make things heavier or lighter just by touching them. Unfortunately, she also gains or depletes her own mass in the process. Cole lured the Torch into a trap, but she later regretted it and turned against her father.

MADAM MEDUSA

Medusa can control every single strand of her living hair and each one is super-strong. Her hair is about 6 feet in length when it's relaxed, but it can stretch to almost three times that length at her mental command. She can snap her hair like a whip and can form it into any solid object that she can imagine. Medusa can also use her hair to perform highly delicate or intricate tasks, such as picking a lock.

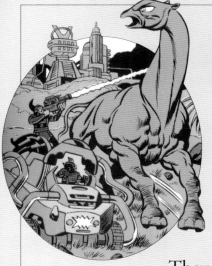

Inhumans

Over 25,000 years ago, aliens known as the Kree visited the Earth, during their endless war with the Skrulls. Though primitive man was just learning how to make fire, the Kree feared that humans might eventually evolve into a powerful race that could be a threat to them. They isolated a small tribe of humans and began to experiment on them, hoping to create an army of super-powerful warriors that would serve their galactic empire. Kree scientists genetically altered the members of this tribe, who became the first Inhumans.

"THE SCIENCE OF *GENETICS* WAS OUR GREATEST INTEREST! WE WERE ABLE, THRU USE OF *VARI-GENES*, TO CONTROL *EVOLUTION* -- AND TO DIRECT IT ANY WAY WE WISHED! WE PRODUCED MANY *INHUMANS* -- ALL WITH SPECIALIZED, CAREFULLY CREATED *SUPER-POWERS!*"

They hide among us

Intending to return sometime in the future to study the results of their experiments, the Kree went back to space, leaving the Inhumans to settle on a tiny island in the Northern Atlantic named Attilan. The Inhumans evolved much faster than their human counterparts and soon became an advanced civilization. They studied genetics and discovered a mutagenic substance called the "Terrigen Mist," which gave them fantastic powers. Ordinary humans grew to fear the Inhumans and their powers and frequently attacked them so the Inhumans tried to avoid humanity and eventually moved Attilan to the Himalayas.

GENETIC ENGINEERING
Using the genetic technology left by the Kree, the Inhumans were able to control the way their species evolved. Many different types of Inhumans were created—in different shapes and sizes, with unique super-powers.

TO THE MOON
After learning that pollution was making his people sick, Black Bolt later moved Attilan from the Himalayas to the Blue Area of the Moon with the help of the Fantastic Four.

Beware the hidden land

The Fantastic Four first met the Inhumans in New York City where they were hiding, and Johnny Storm fell in love with an Inhuman named Crystal. The FF later helped Black Bolt, ruler of the Inhumans, to regain his throne and prevented his brother, Maximus, from destroying humanity. Undaunted by his defeat, Maximus surrounded Attilan with an unbreakable sphere that prevented contact with the outside world. Separated from Crystal, the Torch did everything he could to penetrate the shield but only met with failure. To free his people, Black Bolt used his voice to set off a cataclysmic sonic chain reaction that leveled the entire city as it shattered the barrier.

AND THEN AT LAST, THE INDESCRIBABLE SONIC FORCE STRIKES THE GREAT *BARRIER* ITSELF, CAUSING AN *IMPLOSION* OF SUCH INCALCULABLE POWER THAT IT CANNOT POSSIBLY BE DESCRIBED IN MERELY *HUMAN* TERMS --!

SUFFICE IT TO SAY, THE INCREDIBLE NEGATIVE ZONE VANISHES IN THE SPACE OF A SINGLE HEART-BEAT --AS SUDDENLY, AND INEXPLICABLY AS IT HAD FIRST APPEARED!

Black Bolt

The ruler of the Inhumans, Black Bolt, possesses super-strength and can soar like an eagle. The fork-shaped antenna on his forehead allows him to collect electrons from the air and use them to increase his strength and speed. Unfortunately, Black Bolt must not speak because his voice triggers sonic shockwaves. Even a whisper could demolish an entire city block.

SLOWLY, CALMLY, IRREVOCABLY-- THE SILENT SOVEREIGN *BRACES* HIMSELF --

THEN, WITH HEAD HELD HIGH, HIS MOUTH *OPENS* --

AND THE *VOICE OF BLACK BOLT* IS HEARD THRUOUT THE LAND!

THE ROYAL FAMILY

The royal family of the Inhumans includes Black Bolt's cousins Karnak, Triton, and Gorgon, his wife, Medusa, and her sister, Crystal.

NEVER... WHILE THOSE WHO FOLLOW *BLACK BOLT* LIVE!

CRYSTAL!! NO, YOU FOOL --- NO!

Crystal unleashes her powers.

HOLD HIM THERE, LOCKJAW! DO NOT LET HIM GO! REPEAT -- DO NOT LET HIM GO!

I GOT SOMETHIN' TO SAY ABOUT WHETHER I STAY OR GO, CHARLIE!

WOOOFF!

GORGON
Gorgon's legs can generate powerful seismic tremors.

KARNAK
Karnak can sense an object's weakest point, enabling him to shatter the object with a single blow.

CRYSTAL
Crystal can mentally manipulate the four basic elements: fire, water, earth, and air.

TRITON
Triton is an amphibian with superhuman strength.

LOCKJAW
Crystal's pet and faithful companion, Lockjaw, can teleport himself and anything near him to wherever he wants to go. He is extremely strong and has super-powerful jaws.

Maximus the Mad

Maximus has always been jealous of his older brother, Black Bolt, and has often tried to steal his throne. Thinking the Kree might help him, Maximus once tried to make an alliance with them but Black Bolt put a stop to his plans. Maximus hates the human race and has repeatedly tried to destroy mankind. He secretly loves Medusa and staged his first successful civil war during the time when she had amnesia and Black Bolt was out searching for her. Though he was later overthrown, Maximus has never stopped trying to replace his brother. Maximus also has latent psionic powers, but his mental instability often prevents him from using them. When his powers are operating at peak efficiency, he can control the minds of others and force everyone within his general area to obey his mental commands. He can also blank a person's mind and give them a brief case of amnesia.

SO! THE SILENT ONE DARES RETURN FROM EXILE! THIS TIME BLACK BOLT HAS GONE *TOO FAR!*

Galactus and Silver Surfer

BEFORE THE BIRTH

of the present universe, there was another universe, and the being known as Galactus is its only survivor. Galen was born on a world named Taa, and he knew that his universe was dying. It was collapsing toward a central point called the "Cosmic Egg." It was also releasing lethal radiation that exterminated entire civilizations. Realizing that there was no way to save Taa, Galen decided to drive his starship directly into the heart of the "Cosmic Egg," but instead of serving as his funeral pyre, it somehow absorbed Galen into itself. After an undetermined amount of time, the "Cosmic Egg" underwent the "Big Bang" that created the current universe, and Galen was reborn. He was now Galactus, a creature with incalculable power and a never-ending hunger for energy.

The devourer of worlds

Galactus needs a particular type of energy that can only be found on certain worlds, and he must consume the entire planet to obtain it. He has traveled across the current universe for many millennia, constantly searching for worlds to devour. Galactus possesses cosmic power on an unimaginable scale. He can restructure matter and project an energy blast powerful enough to shatter a medium-sized planet. He can instantly teleport objects across the galaxy and erect invincible force fields. His base of operations is a space station that is as big as an entire solar system. Though Galactus destroys entire planets and has doomed countless civilizations, he considers himself to be far beyond conventional definitions of "good" or "evil."

OUR RACE MUST DIE -- IN A MANNER BEFITTING TAA!

THEN WE MUST PREPARE -- FOR THE INEVITABLE!

IT IS HOPELESS! NOTHING THAT LIVES CAN ESCAPE THE PLAGUE!

MY INCUBATION PERIOD IS ENDED!

GALACTUS LIVES!

Sentinel of the Spaceways

The people of Zenn-La lived in a virtual paradise. War, crime, disease, and poverty had been eliminated long ago. No one had to work, and everything was free. Everyone seemed happy... except for Norrin Radd. He hungered for adventure and yearned to explore the universe. He got his wish the day the planet-wide warning system detected an alien spacecraft headed toward Zenn-La—Galactus had come to feed.

After the planet's defense system failed to drive off the invader, Norrin Radd borrowed a starship and made an offer to Galactus. If he would spare Zenn-La, Norrin agreed to serve Galactus and seek new worlds for him to devour. Galactus gave some of his cosmic power to Norrin Radd and covered Norrin's body with an indestructible silver coating. Galactus also gave his new herald a unique device that resembled an earthly surfboard so that Norrin could travel through space. Thus was born the Silver Surfer.

Though he was bored with life on Zenn-La, Shalla Bal was the great love of Norrin Radd's life.

Befriended by Alicia Masters and impressed by her dignity and compassion, the Surfer tried to save the Earth from Galactus. No matter how far he roams, the Silver Surfer still keeps a close eye on the Earth and has often returned to defend it.

IF THIS BE DOOMSDAY...

The Silver Surfer served Galactus faithfully for many years. While searching for a suitable planet, the Surfer noticed a mass of space debris and discovered that Uatu the Watcher had erected a rocky barrier to conceal the Earth. After signaling Galactus, the Surfer met Alicia Masters, who convinced him that the human race deserved to survive. The Surfer begged Galactus to leave the Earth, and when he refused, the Surfer defied Galactus and joined the battle against him. After yielding to Mr. Fantastic and the Ultimate Nullifier, Galactus punished his former herald by erecting an energy barrier that imprisoned the Surfer on Earth.

BEYOND THE BARRIER

After exile on Earth, the Surfer breached the barrier and was free to roam the cosmos once again. He returned to Zenn-La and learned that Galactus had punished the planet for his betrayal. He granted Shalla-Bal a portion of his cosmic power and left her to restore Zenn-La to its former glory.

Black Panther

T'Challa

The "Black Panther" is an honorary title bestowed on the reigning king of Wakanda.

IN **HIS** attempt to steal precious, energy-absorbing vibranium from the African nation of Wakanda, the evil scientist Ulysses Klaw murdered T'Chaka, the Wakandan chieftain. The ruler's young son, T'Challa, drove Klaw from his lands and became the new king. Educated in the finest schools in Europe and America, he studied physics and became a brilliant inventor. After returning to his homeland, T'Challa resumed his royal duties and donned the mantle of the Black Panther, sacred totem of his people.

Beloved Wakanda

Though he has often allied himself with the Fantastic Four and the Avengers, the Black Panther gives the people of Wakanda his highest priority. T'Challa has faced rivals to his throne, attempts to steal his country's wealth, and invasion threats, but he has defeated them all.

IDOL WORSHIP
Once worshiped as a god, the panther is still a sacred animal to all Wakandans.

The greatest game

T'Challa once invited the FF to Wakanda to join him on a hunt but neglected to say that they would be the prey! He lured them all into different traps to test the limits of their capabilities and to hone his own fighting skills. After the FF escaped these traps, he held a feast for his guests in their honor.

Cat costume

The Black Panther's costume incorporates thin strands of vibranium, expertly woven into the fabric. The energy-absorbing metal causes objects to lose their momentum on contact, making bullets drop to the ground and punches lose their force. The boots of the costume are also constructed from vibranium, making it possible for T'Challa to land on his feet from great heights without harm. His natural night vision is greatly enhanced by special lenses built into the costume, and the fingers of his gloves can expel sleeping gas.

CAT FIGHT

In one encounter, the Black Panther's fighting abilities even enabled him to defeat Reed Richards.

AND, UNLIKE A MERE *HUMAN*, THE CAT IS *NEVER* SIGHTLESS IN THE *DARK*!

UHHHH -- !

MR. FANTASTIC...LEADER OF THE *FANTASTIC FOUR*... HELPLESS BEFORE THE POWER OF THE *BLACK PANTHER* MY HOUR OF *TRIUMPH* AT LAST!

Power to the Panther

Although he doesn't possess any superhuman powers, the Black Panther has the strength and speed of the most gifted Olympic athletes. He is also a highly skilled gymnast and acrobat. Thanks to a special heart-shaped herb found only in Wakanda, his five senses are highly enhanced. He has particularly keen eyesight and night vision. T'Challa is also an accomplished hunter, who can track a quarry across almost any jungle or city terrain. His unique fighting style employs various martial arts along with acrobatics and a number of catlike actions, positions, and blows.

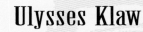

WE DON'T KNOW WHAT'S *UP*, PANTHER - -BUT IT'LL BE MORE FUN FIGHTING *WITH* YOU THAN *AGAINST* YOU!

FLAME ON!

I'VE COME *THIS* FAR WITH THE F.F.- -I MIGHT AS WELL GO *ALL* THE WAY!

IF EVERYONE *ELSE* CAN BE A CORNBALL, SO CAN I! IT'S *CLOBBERIN'* TIME!

THERE IS NO NEED FOR *YOU* TO SHARE THE DANGER! THIS IS A BATTLE FOR THE SON OF *T'CHAKA*!

A LITTLE *ACTION* WILL BE GOOD FOR JOHNNY-- TO STOP HIM FROM BROOD-ING OVER CRYSTAL!

HENCE, I SHALL DON MY RITUALISTIC GARB, AS THE *BLACK PANTHER* STALKS AGAIN!

WAIT FOR *ME*, REED! WHATEVER IS OUT THERE-- WE'LL FACE IT *TOGETHER*!

Sound control

Klaw's transformation into a form of "sonic life" makes him impervious to many of the most powerful weapons designed to immobilize ordinary human beings. His unique ability to transform and control sound also makes him a dangerous adversary. He can project intense high-volume sound waves that are loud enough to shatter steel or fire concussive blasts powerful enough to stun even the Hulk. He can also generate three-dimensional objects that resemble living creatures and obey his mental commands.

Ulysses Klaw

When the scientist Ulysses Klaw designed a device that could transform sound into physical objects, he realized his machine would need vibranium to work. To this end, Kraw traveled to the tiny northern African nation of Wakanda, the world's main supplier of this extremely rare metal. Murdering the chieftain, T'Chaka, in an attempt to steal the vibranium, Kraw was confronted by the Wakandan ruler's young son, T'Challa. Gaining control of Klaw's sound blaster weapon, T'Challa used it to shatter the killer's right hand. Klaw replaced his hand with a new sonic blaster and later altered his entire body into "living sound." He is now able to transform sound into many different weapons.

IT *HAS* TO STOP YOU -- IT *HAS* TO! IT CAN *SHOCK* AND *IMMOBILIZE* THE NERVOUS SYSTEM OF ANY LIVING *HUMAN BEING*!

F-TOOF!

PERHAPS IT *CAN*! BUT YOU HAVE FORGOTTEN *ONE THING* -- ONE *VITAL* FACT -- !

I AM *NO LONGER* A LIVING *HUMAN BEING*! I AM A FORM OF *SONIC LIFE*- -WITH POWER GREATER THAN ANY YOU HAVE EVER *KNOWN*!

Kree Sentry and Ronan

AN EXTRATERRESTRIAL race, the Kree occupy the Greater Magellanic Cloud. This humanoid race created an empire using knowledge acquired from Skrull technology and made the planet of Kree-Lar their capital. Their blue or pink bodies are adapted to conditions on Hala, their planet of origin. However, in order to visit Earth, they don special apparatus that allows them to breathe Earth's atmosphere, and their dense bodies mean that they are twice as strong as the average human. They are ruled by Supreme Intelligence, a vast computer to which all of the Kree intellects are linked. Sentries are employed to watch over member-worlds. Despite being far more technologically advanced than humans, the Kree is aware of the genetic potential of humans and the possibilities available for exploiting it.

Kree–Skrull war

Millions of years ago, the Skrulls landed on the planet Hala, where they found the Kree race and the Cotati race, a group of plantlike entities. The Skrulls sent both races to a barren planetoid to see which group would be worthy of becoming a part of the Skrull empire. Based on the environments each race created, the Skrulls decided that the Cotati were worthiest. In anger, the Kree attacked the Skrull ship. Becoming masters of Skrull technology, the Kree then attacked the Skrull empire. The result was the Kree–Skrull war, which would continue for thousands of years.

SENTRY 459

The second prototype sentry, Sentry 459 traveled to Earth with the Kree where, through a series of genetic experiments, they created the Inhumans. Sentry 459 was ordered to remain on Earth to watch over the new race once the Kree had left. One day, archaeologist Daniel Damian stumbled across Sentry 459 and activated it, resulting in the sentry capturing Damian and sending a report to its masters. The Fantastic Four detected the sentry's surveillance devices and fought and subdued the guard, freeing Dr. Damian. Following the battle, the Kree Accuser, Ronan, traveled to Earth in order to punish those who had defeated Sentry 459.

The 15-foot-tall Sentry 459 was able to blast energy beams out of its eyes. Its strong armor could protect it from beam attacks.

FLAME ON

Johnny Storm fought in the frontline against Sentry 459. After the sentry was defeated, it deactivated itself. Following a brief reactivation, Sentry 459 was destroyed by Ronan. A third sentry was created, Sentry 9168, and the Fantastic Four fought and blew up this Kree guardian.

Ronan the Accuser

The Accusers are an elite group of Kree government officials who enforce justice throughout the Kree Empire. Ronan was the Supreme Public Accuser. Only the Imperial Minister and Supreme Intelligence were above him. After the defeat of Sentry 459 at the hands of the FF, Ronan journeyed to Earth to exact justice.

ACCUSATION
Armed with his Cosmi-Rod that is capable of inflicting unearthly damage, Ronan accuses the FF of depriving the Supreme Intelligence of an invaluable sentry.

ELASTIC FANTASTIC
Despite Ronan's unearthly strength, the Fantastic Four eventually won the battle. The Supreme Intelligence blamed Ronan for losing the fight and merely put Earth under observation rather than trying to make sure that justice was done. This angered Ronan.

Blastaar

The king of planet Baluur in the Negative Zone, Blastaar was a ruthless ruler. His subjects over-threw him and imprisoned him in an adhesion suit, sending him adrift in outer space. Blastaar freed himself and followed Reed Richards to Earth. The Fantastic Four battled Blastaar and sent him back to the Negative Zone, where he reclaimed his throne. However, he has returned to Earth on many occasions, determined to conquer the planet. He wants to shatter the portal between Earth and the Negative Zone so that he can freely move between the two. He has the ability to generate kinetic energy through his fingertips at a range of 1,000 feet. He also uses this skill to propel himself like a rocket.

Power of intelligence

Believing that the Empire should not be ruled by a non-humanoid entity, Ronan joined with Kree Imperial Minister Zarek to overthrow the Supreme Intelligence. However, it found out and imprisoned them. Ronan's allies freed him, and he took control. A Kree–Skrull war broke out, and the Supreme Intelligence regained power. Ronan went mad, but the computer restored Ronan's sanity and allied itself with him again.

WHY AM I *DIFFERENT* FROM THE OTHERS? THEY WATCH ME... AND THEY *HATE* ME, BECAUSE I AM *DIFFERENT*.

WHAT *MAKES* ME *DIFFERENT*? *WHAT*?

"IT WAS HIS VERY ABILITY TO *ASK* THAT QUESTION WHICH ALIENATED HIM..."

Annihilus

OVER A THOUSAND years ago, an alien race attempted to populate the barren worlds in the alternate dimension known as the Negative Zone. They gathered living spores in canisters of power and sent a spaceship to spread the spores across their universe. The ship crashed on Arthos, a planet full of deadly volcanoes and toxic swamps. Knowing their days were numbered, the aliens released the spores, and some of these evolved into brutal monsters. One named Annihilus was an intelligent, insectlike creature who was often attacked by the others.

The living death

Annihilus stumbled upon the spaceship and used the alien technology and canisters of power to build a device called the Cosmic Control Rod. The rod increased his strength and intelligence. He attacked the monsters who had threatened him and set out to conquer the rest of the Negative Zone.

HERE IN MY HANDS...I HOLD THE MOST *PRECIOUS* ITEM IN ALL THE WORLD...

MY LIFE-GIVING... LIFE-PROLONGING *COSMIC CONTROL ROD!*

AND, NOT *MAN* NOR *BEAST* SHALL EVER WREST IT FROM ME!

Let there be life

Reed Richards first encountered Annihilus when he made an emergency voyage to the Negative Zone. With the birth of his son imminent, Reed learned that his wife and their baby were in great danger because the cosmic radiation that had turned Sue into the Invisible Woman could kill them both. Only one element could save them, and Reed needed go into the Negative Zone to find it. He discovered that this element powered the Cosmic Control Rod, and he had to battle Annihilus until he could siphon enough from the rod to save his wife and son. Since that day, Annihilus has hated the FF and has often tried to destroy them.

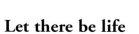

ONLY BY *CRUSHING* ALL WHO LIVE, BE CERTAIN THAT *NONE* WILL EVER THREATEN MY GREATEST *TREASURE!*

THE *TREASURE* WHOSE *COSMIC POWER* HAS EVER GRANTED ME THE PRICELESS GIFT OF... *IMMORTALITY!*

PARANOID
Since the Cosmic Control Rod is the source of his incredible power, Annihilus believes everyone else wants to steal it.

ARMORED INSECTOID
Annihilus wears an armored exoskeleton that protects him from harm, gives him superhuman strength, and allows him to fly at super-speed. The Cosmic Control Rod has stopped him aging, and whilst it is in his possession, Annihilus is immortal. The rod can also fire destructive blasts of incredible force or use cosmic energy to alter matter and change one object into another.

Psycho-Man

MASTER SCIENTIST Psycho-Man rules over Sub-Atomica, a five-planet system within a microscopic universe. When overpopulation threatened the planets, he decided to conquer new worlds and chose the Earth as his first target because its human inhabitants appeared to be particularly susceptible to his highly sophisticated mind-control weapon—the deadly mind-ray.

MIGHTY MACHINE
The giant-sized mind-ray has the potential to control the emotions of every person on Earth.

Divide and conquer

The mind-ray targets victims' emotions, filling their minds with intense feelings of fear, doubt, or hate. The intensity of the emotion is extreme, causing hallucinations and even death from fright because the victim believes that their worst fears have become reality. The Psycho-Man attempted to build a giant mind-ray that could affect the entire Earth. He planned to drive everyone crazy and pit human against human, spreading a plague of hate across the world. Before he could finish the machine, the Fantastic Four teamed up with the Black Panther and the Inhumans and forced him to flee back to his microverse.

With malice toward all

Psycho-Man returned to Earth with an android who used the evil scientist's mind-ray to whip people into a violent frenzy. Sue Richards fell under its power, but Reed later freed Sue, and the FF persued the Psycho-Man to his microverse. The FF were captured but eventually overthrew the Psycho-Man's government and freed Sub-Atomica. Sue later turned the Psycho-Man's mind-ray against him, which drove him insane.

MICROSCOPIC
The Psycho-Man is so minute that he cannot be seen by humans. When he travels to Earth, he wears human-sized battle suits that he controls mentally. The Psycho-Man has a number of different armored suits, and each one possesses specific weapons and abilities.

Him

WITHIN A HIGH-TECH
secret base known as the "Beehive", four scientists
named Dr. Morlak, Dr. Hamilton, Mr. Zota, and Professor
Shinksi pursued their dream of world domination. They
artificially generated a prototype super-being and planned to
duplicate it until they had produced enough superhumans
to form an invincible army, which they would use to take
over the world. However, their heinous plan was ruined
when their creation, known as "Him," became more
powerful than they imagined possible
and turned against its creators,
forcing them to
seek help from
an unlikely
person.

The blind sculptress

Under a false premise, the scientists recruited Alicia Masters
and took her to the Beehive. Their supreme creature emitted
such blinding power that human eyes could not see it. Alicia
was the perfect candidate to locate it because her unseeing
eyes would not be harmed by Him and her renowned ability
as a sculptress would allow them to finally see an exact likeness
of the creature. Equipped with clay, Alicia embarked on her
mission, accompanied by Dr. Hamilton. Within the tunnels
below the complex, the pair faced
many terrifying obstacles but
eventually Him allowed Alicia
to approach, sensing that she
was good. Alicia found the
creature encased within a
cocoon—lonely, afraid,
and about to be "born."

A god in the making

Moments before Him is born, the
Fantastic Four arrive to rescue Alicia
from the Beehive. The scientists are
left anxiously waiting for their creation to emerge from its cocoon,
believing it to be some kind of monster. Him appears as a highly
evolved human and confronts his creators because he knows of
their evil intentions. Determined not to allow the scientists to use
him for ill-purposes, Him summons an enormous amount of
energy and escapes, destroying the Beehive in the process.

*After Him leaves
the Beehive, he
travels to space to
seek his destiny.
Eventually, he
becomes known as
Adam Warlock.*

Torgo

SUPREME WARRIOR Torgo was kidnapped from his home planet of Mekka and taken to Kral, where he was forced to fight as a gladiator in the Great Games by Skrull crime boss Lippy Louie. As a mechanical life-form, Torgo possessed immense strength and so remained unbeaten in the gladiatorial arena for some time. This prompted Louie's rival, Boss Barker, to pay a huge sum to have the Thing captured and brought to Kral in the hope that the orange-skinned fighter would finally defeat Torgo.

Clash of the titans

The battle between the Thing and Torgo was evenly matched. Although the Thing was less experienced in using Skrull weapons, he eventually subdued Torgo. However, he showed mercy toward his foe and let him go. Torgo then managed to overpower the Thing, but he, too, refused to kill his opponent. The Skrulls threatened to destroy Mekka if Torgo did not comply, but luckily the Fantastic Four arrived in time to stop the fight.

On the planet Kral, all the Skrull inhabitants assume the appearance of Prohibition-Era gangsters.

When the Thing was taken to the gladiatorial holding pen to await his battle, he tried to retaliate against the Skrulls, but Torgo warned him that resistance was futile. A deadly Skrull weapon called the Sonic Disruptor was trained upon the home planets of each of the slaves—ready to be fired if they refused to fight.

A slave revolution

The Human Torch destroyed the Skrulls' Sonic Disruptor, and once Mekka was no longer under threat, Torgo led a revolt. The gladiators removed the slave collars that had rendered them helpless for so long and turned against their former masters.

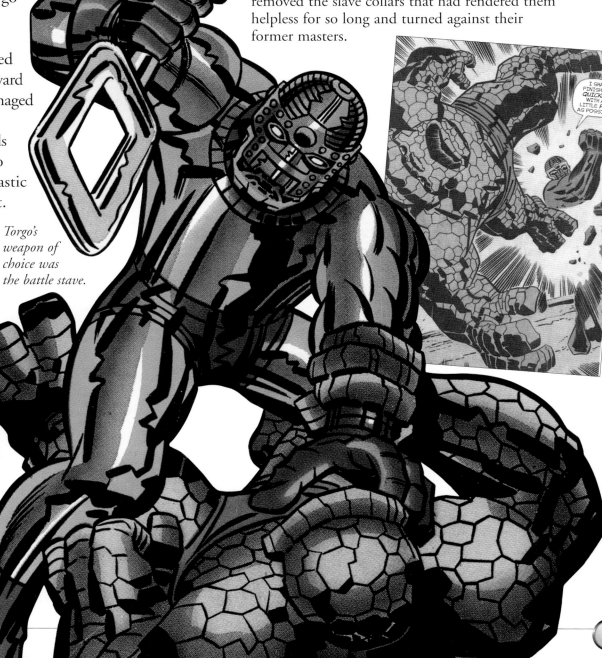

Torgo's weapon of choice was the battle stave.

MISSION TO MEKKA

On a mission to find a potential planet for Galactus to devour, Reed and the Thing arrived on Mekka, where they encountered Torgo once again. Although they assured the Mekkan that they would not allow his planet to be sacrificed, he took them prisoner.

The Fantastic Four in the 1970s

Stan Lee and Jack Kirby celebrated the Fantastic Four's second decade by introducing Agatha Harkness and bringing back the Frightful Four. The Mad Thinker later attacked the FF with his Androids of Death, and the team ran into the Monster from the Lost Lagoon. All good things come to an end, and Jack Kirby left *Fantastic Four* with #102, although an issue that he had partially completed was published about six months later. Artist John Romita took over in the middle of a storyline that featured the Sub-Mariner and Magneto, who normally battled the uncanny X-Men. Romita was followed by John Buscema, Rich Buckler, George Perez, Keith Pollard, and John Byrne. Joe Sinnott, who became Kirby's regular inker with *Fantastic Four #44*, embellished almost every issue in this decade. After a few issues written by Archie Goodwin, Stan Lee turned the FF over to Roy Thomas. Roy replaced Ben Grimm temporarily with Luke Cage and reinstated the Impossible Man after a 12-year absence. Roy was followed by writers Gerry Conway, Tony Isabella, Len Wein, Bill Mantlo, and Marv Wolfman. As the FF grew more popular, Marvel published additional FF-related titles. *Marvel Team-Up* was introduced as a title that would regularly feature Spider-Man and the Human Torch. After a tryout in *Marvel Feature #11*, the Thing began a 100-issue run in *Marvel Two-In-One*. In 1978, the FF got its own animated TV show, with storyboards produced by Jack Kirby and scripts by Roy Thomas.

The Human Torch #1 (Sept. 1974). The Torch gets his own title. (Cover by Sal Buscema)

Fantastic Four #100 (July 1970) The FF celebrate 100 issues by fighting all of their past foes, courtesy of the Mad Thinker and the Puppet Master. (Cover by Jack Kirby)

1970

Fantastic Four #104 (Nov. 1970) The FF battle Magneto. (Cover by John Romita)

1971

Fantastic Four #113 (Aug. 1971) The FF fight the Over-Mind. (Cover by John Buscema)

1972

Fantastic Four #129 (Dec. 1972) The Thing meets Thundra. (Cover by John Buscema)

1973

Fantastic Four #131 (Feb. 1973) Johnny has girlfriend trouble. (Cover by Jim Steranko and Joe Sinnott)

Fantastic Four #191 (Feb. 1978)
Reed Richards resigns and the FF disbands.
(Cover by George Perez and Joe Sinnott)

Fantastic Four #168 (Mar. 1976)
Ben Grimm is replaced by Luke Cage, Power Man. (Cover by Rich Buckler and Joe Sinnott)

1974

Giant-Size Super-Stars *(May 1974) The FF's new quarterly title.*
(Cover by Rich Buckler and Joe Sinnott)

1976

Fantastic Four #171 *(June 1976) The FF meet super-gorilla, Gorr.*
(Cover by George Perez and Joe Sinnott)

1978

Fantastic Four #200 *(Nov. 1978) Reed unmasks Dr. Doom.*
(Cover by Keith Pollard and Joe Sinnott)

1979

Fantastic Four #207 *(June 1979) Featuring Spider-Man.*
(Cover by Keith Pollard and Joe Sinnott.)

NOT AFTER I'VE **INCREASED** THE MASS OF MY ATOMIC STRUCTURE--

BY PRESSING MY CONTROL MODULE TO **HIGHEST INTENSITY.**

SELF-CONTROL
By activating his control module, Nega-Man could fire powerful blasts that were strong enough to knock the Thing out and release tranquilizer mist that would make people unconscious. He traveled in a gyroscopic aircraft that doubled as a battering ram.

Janus the Nega-Man

A SCIENCE MAJOR at college with Reed Richards, Janus started to use his scientific knowledge for negative effect. He was preoccupied with finding a new source of energy, and, when he came across Nega-Power, tried to encourage Reed to help him harness the energy. Reed warned his friend of the dangers if he pursued this negative source but Janus would not listen. Exposed to Nega-Power, Janus split in two—Janus and the Nega-Man, potential master of the world.

YOU WENT ON TO **OTHER** THINGS----BUT I **NEVER** GAVE UP!

THEN, ONE DAY-- THE VERY **POWER** I HAD SOUGHT-- **CHANGED** ME--TURNED ME INTO-- THE **ULTIMATE SCHIZOPHRENIC!**

IT'S LIKE THE LEGEND OF **JEKYLL** AND **HYDE** -- COME TO **LIFE!**

MIRROR IMAGE
Negative energy overtook Janus, and Nega-Man was born. He was the physical manifestation of all that was evil within Janus.

Dominating force

The Nega-Man overpowered Janus and began his bid to rule the world. He robbed a bank but was confronted by the Fantastic Four. The Thing and the Human Torch tried to stop him, while Janus called on Reed for help. Reed made the link between his friend and the Nega-Man and stopped the evil one from using his control module that harnessed negative energy. Janus shot the Nega-Man, and he faded away.

THERE! THERE HE **IS**-- JUST AS I **FEARED!**

IT'S TOO LATE TO **STOP HIM** NOW!

Through the portal

Janus had not learnt his lesson. He gave himself up to the dark urges and became Nega-Man completely. As Janus, he convinced Reed to show him where the portal to the Negative Zone was. In the Distortion Area, he met Annihilus— with explosive results.

WHAT'S **HAPPENING** TO ME? I'M FALLING TOO **FAST! HELP** ME--**HELP!**

YOUR **HAND,** JANUS --REACH OUT TO ME! **REACH** MAN-- **REACH!**

I WANTED **ABSOLUTE** POWER! BUT--NOT LIKE **THIS!**

NOT--LIKE **THIS!**

Out of the world

The Nega-Man agreed to take Annihilus back to the portal in exchange for help to get more Nega-Power. He killed two of Annihilus's servants, but one servant pushed the Nega-Man into the Exploding Atmosphere. Reed could not save him. Janus survived but was later killed trying to get more Nega-Power.

Monster from the Lost Lagoon

THE AMPHIBIOUS Monster and his mate crashed onto Earth deep into the Lost Lagoon. Needing to repair his ship and replace his supply of water, the Monster transformed himself into a human, worked at the Seaquarium, and began attacking ships that came near the lagoon. The Fantastic Four heard of the attacks and boarded their Air-Sea Cruiser. Adopting his human form, the Monster offered to guide the FF through the caves. Once they had traveled deep down into the lagoon, the Monster attacked the FF and fled Earth.

TRANSFORM
The Monster drinks a potion that makes him human. He can understand English but cannot speak it.

CAPTURE
Sue was abducted by the Monster and taken to the bottom of Central Park Lake.

Happy ending

The Monster's mate contracted a terrestrial virus so they were forced to return to Earth to get treatment. The Monster proceeded to abduct Sue Richards. In a bid to escape, she flooded the cavern she was being held in, but the Monster saved her. The Monster said that he needed her help to administer the medication to his mate. Sue helped him, and the Monster and his mate returned to their home planet.

Monocle

SKILLED IN espionage, Monocle used his eyeglass to mesmerize his victims. He also had a camera that was able to blast destructive Neutrak Rays. Attending a UN delegation with the aim of starting World War III, Monocle tested his camera on the Fantastic Four, who were at the meeting. Monocle blasted the Fantasticar out of the sky. Sue and Reed fell into a river, and the Thing and the Human Torch began helping those affected by the blast. Monocle now activated his camera on the UN, but it blew up in his hands—Reed had created a reversal ray.

CHEESE!
Monocle Man's camera hid a powerful Neutrak Ray.

Creating a Storm

Monocle was later employed by the Enclave to help run Security University. Monocle mesmerized student Johnny Storm into stealing weapons secrets from Reed. Spider-Man, who was monitoring the university, told the conscious Johnny what he had been doing. They followed Monocle, and the subsequent chase led to his jet exploding.

Overmind

CREATED BY the Eternals (also known as Eternians) to ensure the survival of their now-extinct race, the Overmind contains the combined mental and physical abilities of a whole civilization. The Eternals chose their greatest warrior, Grom, and imbued him with the mental energy of the entire population. Sent into space, Grom gestated inside a cocoonlike spore for millennia. When he emerged, Grom had transformed into the awesome Overmind. He converted his cocoon into a spacecraft using the power of thought, and set out to continue the Eternals' mission of conquest.

Eternal extinction

A highly advanced race, the Eternals had conquered aging and natural death. Their policy of conquest was a means of population control, as millions of Eternians died in their brutal campaigns. Only one world stood in the way of total Eternian domination—the enormous planet Gigantus. Launching a nuclear attack, the Eternals succeeded only in reducing the planet to huge fragments. The survivors then retaliated, which led to the extinction of the Eternian race and the creation of the Overmind.

Origin of the Overmind

As the survivors of Gigantus attacked Eternus in retaliation for the destruction of their homeworld, Eternian scientists prepared Grom to receive the collective consciousness and mental power of all Eternus. All over the planet, Eternians entered enormous "synthesizing chambers," where their living brains were converted into pure energy and infused into Grom. Possessing the psionic energy of a billion minds and their shared desire for conquest, Grom became "Overmind" of his entire race. Fired into intergalactic space through an interstellar beaming device, he spent eons learning to control his new powers.

ROCK-HIDED DOLT!

WITH BUT THE *MEREST* OF MENTAL COMMANDS—

THE *FLAMING ONE!* YOU ARE *MAD* AS YOUR *COMPANION!*

OF WHAT USE ARE THESE TACTICS WHICH *FAILED* SO MISERABLY BEFORE?

DON'T BE *TOO* CERTAIN WE'RE GOIN' *DOWN,* BIG MAN!

MASTER OF DISGUISE
When Overmind first encountered Earthlings, he realized that his fearsome appearance would attract attention. Using his mental powers, he was able to influence the perception of human beings so that he could blend in among them and walk unnoticed through the city streets. The citizens around him were unaware he was plotting the destruction of the Earth. Only the Fantastic Four knew of his presence, having been forewarned of his plan by the mystical alien entity known as the Watcher. Together, the FF prepared to counter the deadly threat.

BUT, I MUST *SPARE* MYSELF THE INDIGNITY OF YOUR LOATH-SOME *CURIOSITY.*

THUS, WITH A CASUAL *THOUGHT,* I *CHANGE* MY IMAGE IN YOUR EYES

MIND CONTROL

The Overmind's first plan of attack was to use his mind-manipulation powers to turn Reed Richards against the FF. In a dramatic confrontation, Mr. Fantastic battled with the Invisible Girl, the Thing, and the Human Torch before fleeing from the Baxter Building. Reed was then tortured by the Overmind to reveal the FF's plan to defeat him.

"FROM BEYOND THE STARS SHALL COME THE *OVER-MIND*--"

"-- AND HE SHALL CRUSH THE *UNIVERSE!*"

YOU HAVE *HEARD* THAT ANCIENT PROPHECY--

NOW YOU KNOW IT TO BE *TRUE!*

Awesome power

The Overmind is invulnerable to heat, cold, energy, electricity, radiation, toxins, and disease. He does not age and can cast powerful kinetic blasts at his enemies. His telekinetic abilities also enable him to move heavy objects at will. Overmind's mental powers allow him to cast illusions into the minds of his enemies, and so manipulate their thoughts and actions.

YOU WHO ARE CALLED *GENIUS*-- YOU WHO ARE THOUGHT *BRILLIANT* BY THIS SMALL WORLD'S PUNY BEINGS.

WRITHE, REED RICHARDS!

--THE *MENTAL MASTERY* OF THE *OVER-MIND!*

WRITHE BEFORE THE *COMPLETE CONTROL*--

With Mr. Fantastic held captive by the Overmind, the remaining FF joined forces with Doctor Doom to fight the mutual enemy of all humankind. However, their combined powers were not enough to stop him. The Overmind was eventually banished to a lifeless alternate universe by the Stranger, an all-powerful entity whose sole purpose was to hunt and defeat the former Eternal.

GRIMM CAPTIVE

Overmind uses his mental powers to block the Thing's attack.

YOU WILL *NOT* STRIKE AT ME

I--CAN'T MOVE

SLUMPIN'S HOLDIN' ME *BACK*

Air-Walker

When Galactus required a new herald to replace the Silver Surfer, he chose the Xandarian starship captain Gabriel Lan. While traveling home after a seven-year exploratory mission to contact new alien civilizations, Lan encountered the spherical craft of the galaxy-devourer. Galactus, recognizing Lan's desire for unlimited freedom and power, offered him the chance to become the Surfer's successor. Lan accepted and was transformed into the Air-Walker. He spent many years seeking out new planets to sate his master's vast appetite. Air-Walker eventually sacrificed his life to save Galactus, throwing himself in the path of a blast from weaponry built by the Ovoids, a race that feared his master. In gratitude, Galactus transferred Air-Walker's consciousness into a new robotic body.

A NEW HERALD

Reborn as Air-Walker, Lan was granted power over cosmic energy and the ability to travel at hyper-light speeds.

NOW BY MY HAND YOU SHALL BE--

SOON YOU WILL BE *MORE* THAN MORTAL... *MORE* THAN YOU COULD EVER CONCEIVE.

--REBORN!

Arkon The Magnificent

IT'S LIKE... A HOLE IN *SPACE*... AND SOMEONE COMING *THRU* IT..!

BORN INTO nobility in Polemachus, an extra-dimensional world, Arkon's future as a great warrior was inevitable. The humanoids of Polemachus believe that war is the reason for their existence and live for the glory of battle. Named ruler of one of the countries in Polemachus, Arkon set about conquering the rest of his world. However, his plans for overthrow were halted when it was discovered that the planetary rings that provided Polemachus with heat and light were collapsing. The only hope to regenerate the rings was to atomically destroy the Earth, with the resultant energy from such an explosion being transported extra-dimensionally to Polemachus. Arkon would do everything in his power to save his world—regardless of the consequences.

"LET THE BOLD, BRAVE BANNER BE UNFURLED... AND, AT LAST, GREAT ARKON WALK THESE HALLS!"

SOMETHING'S HAPPENING HERE, WITCH... BUT I DON'T KNOW WHAT IT IS!

Earth-bound

Watched by the amphibious Toad, Arkon manipulated the Scarlet Witch to cast a spell on him in order to send him to Earth. Seeing the potential in the witch, Arkon kidnapped her and a group of scientists to help him create an atomic device that he could use on Earth to cause an explosion. But before he could use the device, Iron Man had built a machine that, using Thor's hammer, could reenergize Polemachus's rings. Arkon briefly abandoned his attack on Earth, but it was not enough for the annihilator. He decided that he wanted more atomic power—fast!

AND *WHEN* I SPEAK... LET ALL ELSE KEEP *SILENCE!!*

FOR, I AM HE WHOM *YOU* YOURSELF HAVE SUMMONED WOMAN, FROM MY WORLD BEYOND ALL WORLDS!

I AM *POWER* INCARNATE... THE *LORD* OF WARLORDS... *FIRST* AMONG THE WARRIORS OF A *UNIVERSE!*

I AM... **ARKON THE MAGNIFICENT!!**

Lightning strikes thrice

Arkon is gifted with superhuman strength, dense skin-and-muscle structure capable of withstanding strong attack, and a rate of recuperation faster than average, but his greatest weapons are his lightning bolts. They are solid until they hit the target, when they turn into pure energy. There are three types: the golden bolt opens portals between worlds; the scarlet bolt creates a force equal to ten pounds of TNT; and the powerful black bolt, or D-Bolt, creates a force equal to 20 tons of TNT and can smash mountains!

Three-dimensional

Arkon planned for Earth-A, the Fifth Dimension, and Earth-Prime to fight against each other to provide more energy for Polemachus. The alternate worlds began to merge, and, to everyone's bewilderment, dinosaurs were seen walking in New York City! It was not long before the Fantastic Four arrived on the scene. The Thing brandished a disk that he planned to place in the link between the different worlds to stop Arkon. Obviously prepared to fight Arkon directly, the Thing did not bank on having to confront an agent of Arkon, the skater Gaard.

Darkoth

Desmond Pitt was a US Air Force major when he befriended Ben Grimm. The strength of their friendship was demonstrated when Pitt saved Ben from a potentially fatal plane crash. Pitt was involved in a solar shuttle development project that was infiltrated by Victor Von Doom. Pretending to be Doom's ally, Pitt discovered that the Latverian monarch wanted to use the solar energy for his own country. Eventually, Doom realized Pitt's ruse and replaced his skeleton with steel, mutating him into Darkoth the Death Demon. Using a vibration device, Doom wiped Pitt's memory and made him believe that he was a demon brought to be Doom's warrior. The diabolic creature has fought for and against the Fantastic Four, as he struggles with his role as Doom's pawn.

On Gaard

The super-hockey player Gaard is the Earth-A dimension version of Johnny Storm. In the Earth-A timeline, Johnny was not given super-powers like the others. He was severely injured on the battlefield and was saved by Polemachus scientists, who rebuilt him as an agent of Arkon. When the Thing arrived at the nexus to insert the disk, he was confronted by Gaard. Hearing of this, Reed Richards projected an image of the Thing to distract Gaard. The skater fell for it, and the Thing managed to insert the disk and stop Arkon from getting the explosive ending he desired.

Darkoth's talons can rip through any material, most notably the Thing's rocklike hide.

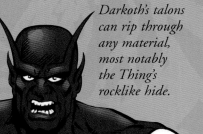

Gaard defended the dimensional gateways for his master, Arkon.

Ironically, the Thing was forced to fight Johnny Storm, though Johnny was in the guise of Gaard. Using his skates to steer through space, Gaard was also given a Cosmic Sceptre, which fired dangerous electronblasts and was an effective deflector of enemies, so long as they were not mere projections!

Thundra

A PRODUCT OF genetic engineering from an alternate-Earth future, Thundra is the most powerful warrior in a world where women are the dominant gender. In this future, the Earth is called Femizonia, and men are systematically oppressed by females, who see them as a threat to the survival of the species. Warriors from Machus, a separate, violent, male-dominated alternate-Earth future, have crossed over the dimensional gap into Femizonia, inciting rebellion in the male population. In a bid to eliminate the very existence of Machus by establishing female superiority once and for all, Thundra was chosen to travel back in time to the present to seek out and defeat the Earth's most powerful man.

"*I* COME FROM A *FUTURE,* MEDUSA-- ONE WHICH WOULD BE *A NIGHTMARE* TO MEN OF YOUR TIME!

Frightful allies

When she arrived on present-day Earth, Thundra initially joined the Frightful Four to assist them in their attempt to acquire the FF's technology. Motivated by the opportunity to fulfil her mission by battling with Ben Grimm, one of the world's most powerful men, she was eager to take on the Fantastic Four. In her first battle against the Thing, she managed to wrap a chain around him and swing the rocky giant into the ground, incapacitating him. Thundra eventually turned against the Frightful Four when she realized the Wizard and his cohorts were prepared to harm Sue Richards' son Franklin in order to achieve their aims. The Femizon subsequently battled against the Thing on numerous occasions, eventually developing strong feelings for her orange-skinned adversary.

...AN *EXAMPLE* IS MADE!

YOU MUST GO BACK INTO THE *PAST,* THUNDRA--

--THERE, TO FIND AND BATTLE THE EARTH'S MOST *POWERFUL MAN*--

THE BESTIAL *THING*-- OUR *CAPTIVE,* AT LAST!

I MUST *SAVOR* THIS MOMENT OF MOMENTS!

DO NOT SAVOR IT *OVERLONG,* WIZARD!

THE *NIGHT* GROWS NEARLY AS SHORT AS MY *PATIENCE.*

FALLEN HERO
Catching Ben Grimm off guard, Thundra managed to beat the Thing in their first encounter. It was to be the first of many such battles.

SUPREME WARRIOR
A martial-arts expert, Thundra is also schooled in politics and military leadership. Her weapon of choice is a chain, which she wields with deadly precision.

Fight of the century

On one occasion, Thundra battled the Thing at Shea Stadium on New Year's Eve. In the presence of many newspaper journalists and television crews and a referee appointed by the city Mayor, the show was billed as the "Fight of the Century." The fight was a sellout, with odds being taken on the victor. Believing herself to be stronger than any man, Thundra was determined to prove her superiority in public. However, the crowds were disappointed when the two combatants eventually decided to leave the stadium to settle the fight privately elsewhere.

YOU STILL DON'T *REALIZE*-- THUNDRA IS STRONGER THAN *YOU*--

--SHE IS STRONGER THAN *ANY MAN ALIVE!*

OOOCH!

AND I INTEND TO *EXPOSE* YOUR PITIABLE MALE INFERIORITY--

-NOW!

UH-*NUH.*

SOME DAYS IT JUST DON'T *PAY* TA GET OUTTA BED

ANSWER ME *NOW,* AND MAYBE I'LL SPARE YOUR MISERABLE *HIDE!*

RESIST ME--AND I'LL TEAR YOU LIMB FROM *LIMB!*

WHERE IS THE SHE-WITCH *THUNDRA?*

BATTLE OF EQUALS

Thundra's frequent battles with the Thing usually ended in stalemate. She also came to realize that her actions on present-day Earth would not prevent the creation of Machus.

MACHUS MAN

Mahkizmo's powers include superhuman strength, the ability to release explosive force from his body, and formidable combat skills.

HE SEES *MAHKIZMO...*

...AND MAHKIZMO SEES *HIM.*

I WANT *THUNDRA,* MALE-LING. GIVE HER TO ME. *NOW.*

SURVIVING SPIRIT

Although he overpowered the FF in their first battle, Mahkizmo was eventually defeated. Surviving the energy implosion, his life-force later took over a new body on the merged world of Machus/Femizonia.

WHIP ME IF YOU *CAN,* ANIMAL.

THERE ISN'T A MALE *ALIVE* WHO CAN DEFEAT *THUNDRA*--

LEAST OF ALL-- *SCUM* LIKE *YOU!*

Enter Mahkizmo

To counter the threat posed by the Femizons in sending Thundra back in time, the Machans sent their own emissary to the present—a warrior named Mahkizmo. He overpowered the FF and used a will-sapping machine on Thundra to teleport her back to Machus. Following Mahkizmo in Doctor Doom's time machine, the FF eventually defeated him with the assistance of the Femizons. In a final battle, the Human Torch and the Thing attacked the Machan as he was summoning the energy for a nuclear-punch. This caused an energy implosion, disintegrating Mahkizmo and causing the alternate worlds of Machus and Femizonia to merge, ending the hostilities.

Crusader Legacy

"URANUS! A GIANT PLANET NEARLY *TWO BILLION MILES* FROM EARTH...

"A COLD, *FORBIDDING* WORLD, RECEIVING ONLY 1/350TH THE HEAT AND LIGHT THAT *EARTH* DOES.

"...YET HOME OF A *SUPER-CIVILIZATION* SO OLD IT HAD FORGOTTEN ITS OWN *DIM ORIGINS!*

"ITS PEOPLE *WELCOMED* MY FATHER--AND FOUND THAT, FOR ALL THEIR SCIENCE, THERE STILL WAS MUCH HE COULD *CONTRIBUTE* TO THE PEACE AND PROSPERITY...

"IN TIME, I *RETURNED* TO EARTH FOR A WHILE...

"...FIGHTING EVIL WITH MORE *PRIMITIVE* WRIST-BANDS WHICH MERELY *BLINDED* MY FOES."

"THEY CALLED ME-- *MARVEL BOY.* *

* AS TOLD IN *MARVEL BOY* AND *ASTONISHING,* CIRCA 1950-1951...AND REPRINTED IN THE LATE 60'S.--ROY.

DR. HORACE GRAYSON fled Germany while Adolf Hitler was still increasing his power. Fearing that a world war was inevitable, the widowed scientist went to America, where he began working on building a private spacecraft. He planned to orbit the moon with his infant son Robert until it was safe to return to Earth. After learning that an advanced civilization was living on Uranus, Grayson headed toward the colony. The Uranians welcomed the father and son and taught Robert all their knowledge. When he became a teenager, Robert decided to visit the Earth and fight crime as the hero called Marvel Boy.

Horrible homecoming

With a gift from the Uranians, a pair of wristbands that could manipulate gravity and emit blinding light, Marvel Boy became a Super Hero. After some time on Earth, he learned that his father was dying on Uranus. Robert tried to borrow money from Calvin McClary, an old friend of his father, for medical supplies. McClary refused, causing Robert to delay his trip. By the time Robert returned to Uranus, an unknown disaster had killed everyone.

MARVEL COMICS GROUP
25¢ 165
THE WORLD'S GREATEST COMIC MAGAZINE!
FANTASTIC FOUR

Convinced that he could have saved his father and the Uranians if his trip had not been delayed, Robert returned to Earth on a mission of vengeance.

NO, YOU GIMPERING CLOWN-- NOT THE *DEVIL!* QUITE THE *OPPOSITE!*

I, MORE THAN *ANY,* AM ON THE SIDE OF THE *ANGELS!*

LOOK! UP THERE-- ON TOP OF THE *ARCH--!*

WHO THE DEVIL IS *THAT?*

STOP HIM! WITH POWER LIKE HIS, HE COULD *DESTROY THE WORLD!!*

CALL HIM CRUSADER

Renaming himself the Crusader, Robert vowed to fight against evil on Earth. His first target was Calvin McClary, whom Robert held responsible for the destruction Uranus.

Rip Van Rampage

On his return to Earth, Robert's ship passed through the tail of a comet and the radiation froze him in a state of suspended animation. He did not awake until his ship crash-landed on Earth decades later. Robert was still determined to get his revenge. He tracked down McClary, murdered him, then went on a rampage and tried to destroy McClary's financial empire. The Fantastic Four tried to stop Robert, but his new wristbands drew their power from the sun and made him virtually unbeatable.

BETTER BANDS

Unlike his original wristbands, Robert's new quantum-bands could manipulate energy over the electro-magnetic spectrum. Responding to his mental commands, they could project and control gravitons (subatomic particles that carry the force of gravity). This enabled Robert to emit concussive blasts and fly.

SUPER-CHARGED

The new quantum-bands could generate a protective invisible energy field that increased Robert's strength to superhuman levels and made him resistant to any form of injury. Neither bullets nor the Torch's flame could harm him.

A new crusade

During his battle with the FF, Robert increased his power, drawing so much solar energy that his quantum-bands overloaded and disintegrated him. Reed Richards took temporary custody of the quantum-bands. After examining them, he gave them to SHIELD, a worldwide intelligence and peacekeeping organization. Dr. Gilbert Vaughn was placed in charge of the bands. His son Wendell was training to be a SHIELD agent so Dr. Vaughn used him to test the bands' powers. To Wendell's surprise and dismay, they became bonded to his wrists forever.

A reluctant Super Hero, Wendell first called himself Marvel Man, then changed his name to Quasar.

Recommended by Captain America, Wendell became the chief of security for Project Pegasus, a top-secret energy research facility where he became friendly with Ben Grimm. Later, Wendell rented a Baxter Building office and became a protector of the universe.

QUASAR

Although these are the same quantum-bands that were worn by Robert, Quasar uses them in different ways. He has developed the ability to create solid objects out of energy. These objects form at the speed of thought and can assume any shape that he can visualize. Quasar can also project beams of concussive force and can fly by surrounding himself with an energy field, moving at the speed of light.

The Brute

The Brute is the Reed Richards of Counter-Earth, a replica of this planet that was positioned so that it would always be in orbit on the far side of the sun. When his world was threatened by a cosmic menace, the alternate Reed rocketed into space to save his planet. He was exposed to cosmic rays and was able to transform himself into a super-strong monster with enhanced, animal-like senses. He eventually landed on the real Earth and was recruited by the Frightful Four. After capturing and trapping the real Reed in the Negative Zone, the Brute tried to take Mr. Fantastic's place, but Sue Richards realized he was an imposter. The real Reed was rescued, and the Brute replaced him in the Negative Zone.

Salem's Seven

HIDDEN AMID the Rocky Mountains is a town named New Salem, whose inhabitants all practice magic. New Salem's citizens isolated themselves from the rest of the world for fear of being persecuted for being witches and warlocks. The leader of the town was a powerful sorceress named Agatha Harkness. Her malevolant son was a warlock called Nicholas Scratch. When Agatha left New Salem for a time to become the governess of Sue and Reed Richards' son Franklin, Nicholas took control of the town and employed his seven children as his private guards, who became known collectively as Salem's Seven.

Power-hungry Nicholas Scratch longed to depose his mother so he could have control of New Salem.

Here there be witches

As citizens of New Salem, the members of Salem's Seven are normal human beings who can wield magic, but unlike the other townsfolk, they also have the ability to magically alter themselves to gain additional superhuman powers and different physical forms. Brutacus can become a man-beast; Gazelle is a super-gymnast who is almost as agile as Daredevil; Hydron can project blasts of water from his left arm; Reptilla becomes a snakelike creature; Thornn can shoot explosive thornlike objects from his body; Vakume can drain energy from anything nearby and can create vacuums; and Vertigo can make people feel dizzy and lose their balance.

Trials and tribulations

Nicholas convinced the people of New Salem that Agatha's contact with the Fantastic Four had betrayed their existence to the outside world, and, therefore, she was guilty of treason. He kidnapped Agatha and Franklin and took them to New Salem so his mother could stand trial. She was found guilty and sentenced to death. The FF tracked them down but were also captured. They later escaped and had to battle Salem's Seven before they could rescue Franklin and stop Agatha's execution. The New Salemites realized that they were wrong about Agatha and exiled Nicholas to another dimension. Salem's Seven have often tried to free their father, but the FF have always stopped them.

"MY JEWEL OF LIFE-- MY KA-STONE-- WOULD NOT LET ME DIE, THUS DID I TAKE LEAVE OF MAN AND BANISH MYSELF TO THE SNOW-CAPPED HIMALAYAS.

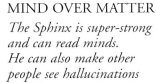

The Sphinx

ONCE THE chief wizard in an ancient Egyptian court, The Sphinx was exiled for displeasing his pharaoh. He wandered the desert for years before stumbling on an abandoned temple. There he found a magic jewel called the Ka stone. He raised the stone to his forehead, where it attached itself, giving him superhuman powers and making him immortal. The Sphinx wandered the Earth for over 5,000 years but grew bored. He tried to free himself from the stone but kept failing. Then he learned of a giant, living computer on an alien world called Xandar that he hoped would possess the knowledge he needed to remove the stone and put an end to his immortality.

If this be my destiny...

The Fantastic Four had come to Xandar to save it from a Skrull invasion. While the FF battled the attackers, the Sphinx became one with the living computer and absorbed all its knowledge and power. He also gained vast cosmic powers and grew to enormous size. Abandoning his plans to commit suicide, the Sphinx decided to conquer the Earth or destroy it.

YIKES! YA GRABBED MY HAND! I -- I CAN'T EVEN BUDGE IT!

HOW'RE YA DOIN' IT? YER NOT EVEN SWEATIN'?

HAVE YOU FORGOTTEN? I AM THE SPHINX! I POSSESS THE POWER OF THE KA STONE... THE STONE OF LIFE ITSELF!

When titans clash

Realizing that they did not have enough power to stop the Sphinx, the FF turned to the only one who could—Galactus! They made a deal with the world-devourer, releasing him from his promise to spare the Earth, in exchange for his help. Not only did Galactus defeat the Sphinx, but he shattered the Ka stone and sent the former wizard back to the past to relive his life over and over again in an endless "time loop."

SURELY THIS WORLD, EARTH, CAN NOT HAVE ANY *HOLD* ON YOU.

REBUKE IT, LET THIS PLANET FALL TO THE SPHINX!

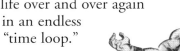

NO!

MIND OVER MATTER

The Sphinx is super-strong and can read minds. He can also make other people see hallucinations and fire concussive bolts of energy from the Ka stone.

Terrax the Tamer

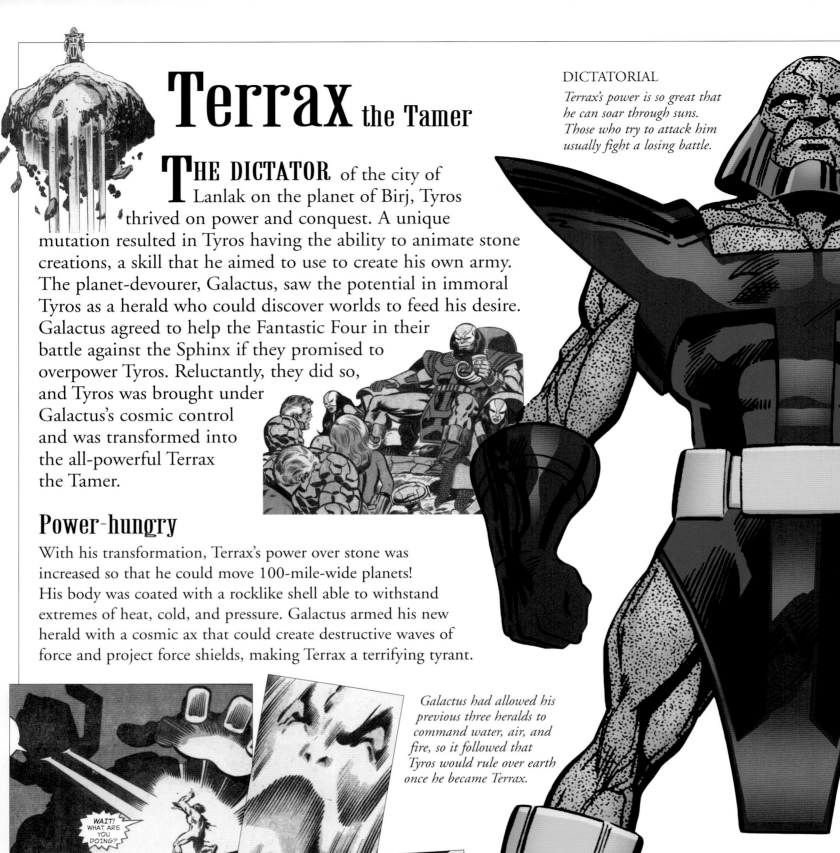

THE DICTATOR of the city of Lanlak on the planet of Birj, Tyros thrived on power and conquest. A unique mutation resulted in Tyros having the ability to animate stone creations, a skill that he aimed to use to create his own army. The planet-devourer, Galactus, saw the potential in immoral Tyros as a herald who could discover worlds to feed his desire. Galactus agreed to help the Fantastic Four in their battle against the Sphinx if they promised to overpower Tyros. Reluctantly, they did so, and Tyros was brought under Galactus's cosmic control and was transformed into the all-powerful Terrax the Tamer.

Power-hungry

With his transformation, Terrax's power over stone was increased so that he could move 100-mile-wide planets! His body was coated with a rocklike shell able to withstand extremes of heat, cold, and pressure. Galactus armed his new herald with a cosmic ax that could create destructive waves of force and project force shields, making Terrax a terrifying tyrant.

Betrayal

Just as he lacked morality, Terrax lacked loyalty, and he conquered planets entirely for his own use. However, Terrax was fearful of Galactus and returned to him. This changed when Terrax fled to Earth and took Manhattan hostage, demanding that the FF destroy Galactus's ship. Galactus removed Terrax's powers and threw him off the top of the World Trade Center tower.

DICTATORIAL
Terrax's power is so great that he can soar through suns. Those who try to attack him usually fight a losing battle.

Galactus had allowed his previous three heralds to command water, air, and fire, so it followed that Tyros would rule over earth once he became Terrax.

WAIT! WHAT ARE YOU DOING?

HE SETTLES ATOP ONE OF THE TALLEST BUILDINGS IN THE WORLD...

FOR A MOMENT HE STANDS STILL, AS IF LISTENING...

LET THE POWER FLOW FROM ME! LET THE WILL OF TERRAX BE FELT!

Atop a Manhattan skyscraper, Terrax displays his might. It is this power that he calls on to levitate the whole of the island of Manhattan. He hopes to strike fear into the FF so that they will help him be free of Galactus.

Return to Tyros

Terrax remained in a coma for several months. He was discovered by Doctor Doom, who believed Terrax would be the ideal candidate to assist him in destroying the Fantastic Four. Doom kidnapped Terrax and helped him recover. Terrax had no memory of being Galactus's herald and reverted to the name of Tyros. Now powerless, Tyros agreed to wear a special suit that Dr. Doom had created, which would harness and regulate his cosmic energies. Little did Tyros know that these cosmic powers would work against him and eventually consume him.

BUT IT IS, FOOL! IT IS!! THOUGH YOU MAY HAVE THOUGHT ME DEAD BY THE HAND OF WORLD-DEVOURING GALACTUS, I AM RISEN, MORE POWERFUL THAN EVER I WAS BEFORE!

NOW AND FOREVER MORE I AM TYROS THE TERRIBLE!

DOOM'S IN ON THIS, TOO? WHAT IS THIS, NATIONAL TROMP THE FF WEEK?

THIS WHOLE ATTACK WAS DOOM'S PLAN, BEN. HE'S THE ONE WHO BROUGHT TYROS BACK!

YEAH? WELL THEM TWO DON'T LOOK NONE TOO BUDDY-BUDDY TA ME!

Cosmic conflict

Tyros was eager to help Doom for personal reasons. In the past, Tyros had been humiliated in front of his people when the Fantastic Four defeated him and took him to Galactus—he wanted revenge. Tyros defeated the FF, and then channeled his anger toward Doctor Doom, enraged at being under his control. Having disabled Doom, Tyros thought victory was within his grasp, but at that moment, Galactus's first herald, the Silver Surfer, arrived, saved the FF, and overwhelmed Tyros. The cosmic power within Tyros's special suit depleted him, and he went into hiding, weak and ruined.

INDEED, DOOM IS UNLEASHING THE FULL MIGHT OF HIS ARMORED BATTLE SUIT AGAINST HIS ERSTWHILE "PARTNER"

IGNORANT ALIEN SAVAGE! I AM DOOM! THIS IS MY PLAN! MY VICTORY! WITHOUT THE DEGRADATION OF REED RICHARDS IT WOULD MEAN NOTHING!

YEARRGH!

Both Tyros and Doctor Doom want to triumph over the Fantastic Four. After Tyros has defeated the FF, the two power-mad figures fight it out over whose victory it will be!

HERBIE

Using technology supplied by the living computers of the planet Xandar, Reed Richards created HERBIE (Humanoid Experimental Robot, B-Type, Integrated Electronics) to help locate Galactus. The robust robot could launch paralyzing opti-blasts and use his retractable tendrils to access computers. However, HERBIE had been possessed by the evil Dr. Sun. He tapped into the Baxter Building computer to get information on the Fantastic Four, which allowed him to find and attack the team. Abandoned by Sun, HERBIE slammed into a computer, destroying himself and Sun in order to save the FF.

BLASTOFF
Sue Richards' usually strong force fields are no match for HERBIE's overwhelming opti-blasts.

H-HE'S RIGHT! STRAIN IS UN-BEARABLE! I'VE GOT TO DROP MY FORCE FIELD--

The Fantastic Four in the 1980s

Writer Marv Wolfman and artist John Byrne launched the new decade by having the Human Torch save his teammates from the effects of a Skrull Aging Ray. Blastarr later returned and a god took a stroll down New York's Times Square. Writer Doug Moench and artist Bill Sienkiewicz then took over. They brought back the Sub-Mariner and Salem's Seven and made the Avengers guest-stars. *The Fantastic Four #232* was called "Back to Basics." It signaled the beginning of an acclaimed run by writer and artist John Byrne.

Fantastic Four #252 (March 1983)
As the FF enter the Negative Zone, their whole world is literally turned on its side when John Byrne produces Marvel's first sideways comic book. (Cover by John Byrne)

He reintroduced Diablo, gave Sue a new hairdo, sent Johnny on a mission for a dead man, and had the FF save the Earth from Ego, the living planet. A triple-sized 20th Anniversary special featured "Terror In A Tiny Town" and a Stan Lee story developed from old storyboards drawn by Jack Kirby. During the course of the next few years, Byrne moved the Inhumans to the Moon, sent the FF into the Negative Zone for six issues, had Annihilus attack the Earth, and Dr. Doom was apparently destroyed—his heir, Kristoff, becoming the new Doom. Byrne also replaced Ben Grimm with the She-Hulk, had Sue change her name to the Invisible Woman, exchanged the Baxter Building for Four Freedoms Plaza, and ignited Johnny Storm and Alicia Masters' romance. After Byrne left, Roger Stern and John Buscema had Johnny and Alicia marry. Steve Englehart and Keith Pollard gave Reed and Sue leave, bringing in Crystal and the She-Thing. As the decade ended, Walt Simonson took over as the new writer.

Fantastic Four #214
(Jan. 1980) Only Johnny Storm can save the FF. (Cover by John Byrne)

1980

Fantastic Four #220 (July 1980)
A monochromatic cover celebrates the first issue written by John Byrne. (Cover by John Byrne and Joe Sinnott)

1981

Fantastic Four #236 (Nov. 1981)
Stan Lee and Jack Kirby help the FF celebrate their 20th anniversary. (Cover by John Byrne and Terry Austin)

1982

Fantastic Four #238 (Jan. 1982)
Johnny Storm learns there is something special about his new girlfriend. (Cover by John Byrne)

1983

Fantastic Four #250 (Jan. 1983)
The 250th issue features Spider-Man and Skrulls imitating the X-Men. (Cover by John Byrne and Terry Austin)

THE WORLD'S GREATEST COMIC MAGAZINE!

Fantastic Four

Hey guys, I know it's Assistant Editor Month, but let's not do anything too silly on the cover—okay? Love & Kisses John

THE TRIAL OF REED RICHARDS

Fantastic Four #317 (Aug. 1988)
With Reed and Sue on temporary leave, a recently mutated Ben leads an all-new team that consists of the Human Torch, Crystal, and the She-Thing. (Cover by Ron Frenz and Joe Sinnott)

Fantastic Four #262 (Jan. 1984)
Reed Richards must defend his decision to save the life of Galactus. (Cover by John Byrne)

1984

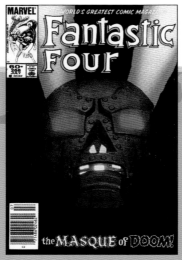

Fantastic Four #268 (July 1984)
Dr. Doom was apparently killed eight issues ago, yet his mask suddenly attacks everyone's favorite foursome. (Photo cover)

1985

Fantastic Four #275 (Feb. 1985)
A sleazy publisher prints photographs of the She-Hulk sunbathing. (Cover by John Byrne and Al Gordon)

1986

Fantastic Four #296 (Nov. 1986)
Stan Lee returns to script a triple-sized spectacular that commemorates 25 years of Fantastic Four.

1989

Fantastic Four #334 (Dec. 1989)
The Fantastic Four fight a host of deadly Super Villains. (Cover by Walt Simonson)

Nova

THE ADOPTED daughter of William

Raye, aka Phineas T. Horton, 14-year-old Frankie Raye became Nova in a freak accident. Horton had invented the android Human Torch, a crimefighter active in the 1940s and 50s. When the FF's Johnny Storm took the name of his now-obsolete creation, Horton was incensed. During Horton's attempt to reactivate his android, Frankie was exposed to the chemicals he had used to construct it, instantly gaining its powers.

Torched memories

The fiery chemicals that engulfed Frankie in Horton's lab gave her the ability to create and control flame without harming herself. Wracked with guilt, Horton hypnotized Frankie, blocking all memory of the event and her new capabilities and giving her a fear of fire. However, Frankie felt herself strangely drawn to Johnny Storm and began dating him. This led to the sudden, shock return of her memory and ability to "flame-on."

I— REMEMBER!

FRANKIE!

Full control

Frankie's new powers were very similar to those possessed by Johnny Storm. While Johnny could achieve higher temperatures and flying speeds, Frankie could maintain her flames longer and had more precise control over the range of temperatures she could reach.

ART FAIRS-- ROCK JOINTS -- YOU SURE LIVE IN A *SWINGIN'* PART OF TOWN FRANKIE!

WHERE DO *YOU* HANG YOUR NON-EX-ISTENT HAT...

WHAT ABOUT *YOU* MYSTERY MAN!

"WHAT HAPPENED THEN WAS... WELL, A *MIRACLE!* THE FLAMES WERE ALL OVER ME, INSIDE ME, LIKE LIVING THINGS, AND YET, THERE WAS NO PAIN, NO SENSATION OF BURNING! IN FACT, SOME-

HOW I SENSED THAT ALL I'D HAVE TO DO TO STOP THE FLAME WAS... THINK IT!

Flying free

After breaking through the memory blocks placed by her stepfather, Frankie Raye experimented with her powers. Soaring over the skyscrapers of Manhattan, she was followed by Johnny, who warned of the dangers posed by her abilities. Following tests at the Baxter Building, Raye was offered the chance to join the FF.

In order to become a fully fledged member of the Fantastic Four, Frankie had to undergo intensive training to control her powers.

Herald of Galactus

Although she enjoyed her work with the Fantastic Four, Frankie was restless, desiring more "cosmic grandeur." When Galactus threatened Earth, she offered to become his new herald in exchange for sparing the planet. Transformed into Nova, her new cosmic abilities gave her power equivalent to that of a miniature sun, while being able to travel at light speed through space satisfied her desire for freedom.

Ego, the Living Planet

One of the strangest phenomenons in the universe, Ego is a sentient world. Also known as the Living Planet, Ego formed from coalescing gas and dust in the same way as other worlds. Over the eons, it developed consciousness and intelligence, eventually creating powerful humanoids out of its own material to conquer other planets. After an encounter with Galactus, Ego was equipped with a propulsion unit. Using its psionic powers to control the device, the power-crazed planet traveled to Earth. Its gravitational forces had a devastating effect, but the FF in turn trapped Ego in the Sun's gravitational field, causing it to disintegrate.

Terminus

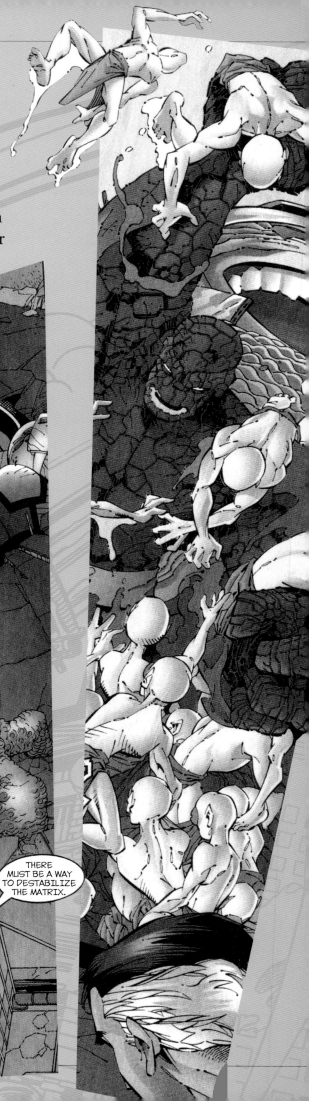

POSSESSING incalculable strength, the massive destroyer Terminus is one of the Fantastic Four's most formidable foes. The scavenger's sole purpose in life seems to be stripping planets of their elements for his own use. He plunders advanced technology from the worlds he attacks and makes slaves of their inhabitants. Terminus is almost indestructible—he takes no time at all to recover from even the most devastating blow—and can even survive being sent to Earth's core.

"A CULTURE OF TINY *MICROBES*-- A NEW FORM OF LIFE NOT BASED ON CARBON.

"THEY CALL THEM *TERMINI*--

"--FOR THEY ARE MEANT TO BRING THE *END* OF THE CELESTIALS' DREAM OF A STRUCTURED, PEACEFUL UNIVERSE.

Instrument of revenge

Terminus was the terrible invention of an alien race destroyed for its sins by the Celestials, a race of super-giants. On the point of their destruction, the aliens created a culture of tiny microbes that eventually evolved into Terminus. As their avenger, he traveled from world to world, destroying any planet spared by the Celestials.

Almost unstoppable

The mighty Terminus's armor is made of living metal. It is able to withstand incredible forces but can be breached. Should he need to, Terminus can regenerate any injured or missing body parts. But his destructive power comes from his mighty energy lance. The 240-foot lance can strip planets of their energy and create atomic storms.

THERE MUST BE A WAY TO DESTABILIZE THE MATRIX.

TERMINATION
The Fantastic Four square up to Terminus.

Stopping the scavenger

In spite of his size and power, Terminus's first Earth invasion was halted by Mr. Fantastic and She-Hulk. They knocked the scavenger's lance from his grasp and sent him to Earth's fiery core. Terminus survived the molten rock, but without his lance, it took him months to climb back to the surface. On another occasion, a formless Terminus returned to Earth and traveled to Subterranea. There, he took over the Moloid Subterraneans—he wanted to use them to make himself a new body. A team of Super Heroes that included the Fantastic Four joined forces with Mole Man to rescue the Moloids and leave Terminus without a body.

LET NO MORE TIME BE WASTED! TERMINUS HAS CROSSED THE GREAT GULF IN SEARCH OF SPOILS!

LET TERMINUS NOW BE SATISFIED!

Gladiator

The mohican-haired alien Gladiator is praetor (leader) of the Shi'ar Imperial Guard. This elite force protects the empress of the Shi'ar Empire. He first encountered the Fantastic Four when he mistook them for evil Skrulls. Gladiator possesses amazing strength and proved it by lifting the 35-story Baxter Building without it collapsing. His body is virtually invulnerable, and he can fly at light speed. During his battle with the Fantastic Four, he beat the Thing and the Human Torch but was made helpless when Mr. Fantastic figured out a way to neutralize his powers. Gladiator later joined forces with the Fantastic Four to defeat a dreaming Celestial.

DID I TRAVEL A HUNDRED LIGHT YEARS FOR SUCH PITIFUL PLUNDER?

WELL? DID I?!?!

GREAT ONE... PLEASE...

YOU WERE SO KEEN TO LEAVE ARIANIS MAJOR... IN SUCH A GREAT RUSH TO GET ON TO THE NEXT WORLD...

YOU GAVE ME INSUFFICIENT TIME TO ESTIMATE THE PRECISE NATURE OF...

Earth is next

Terminus was first persuaded to go to Earth by an alien scientist that he had enslaved. The scientist hoped that Earth's Super Heroes could stop the destroyer. Terminus sent an energy beam from space to carve a message on Earth's surface. The giant beam hit the continental United States, creating words that stretched across the country. They read, "I claim this world—Terminus."

MIND GAMES

If Gladiator begins to doubt himself, his powers are affected. Mr. Fantastic uses this vulnerability to block the alien's attack on the Fantastic Four.

WORDS! WORDS WORDS WORDS! TERMINUS HAS NO TIME FOR WORDS, NO TIME FOR EXCUSES. TERMINUS HAS TIME ONLY FOR WEALTH, FOR LOOT AND POWER!

YOU HAVE FAILED ME, SLAVE!

ENOUGH PURE BRUTE FORCE TO LAY LOW A CITY CRASHES AGAINST THE MOCKING FIGURE BEFORE HIM.

Last words

Terminus was displeased with Earth, and in his anger, he mortally wounded the alien scientist. With his dying breath, the enslaved alien told the Fantastic Four of the danger Earth faced.

GREAT ONE! NO! NO!

Malice
The Mistress of Hate

SHORTLY AFTER Kristoff Vernard masqueraded as Doctor Doom and blew up the Baxter Building, the Fantastic Four returned to the site of their former headquarters. While Reed conferred with the police, another former tenant arrived. Mr. Shoenstein had a snack shop in the building for 22 years and was angry over the loss of his business. Reed tried to calm him, but the police overreacted and slammed the old man against a wall. She-Hulk and Wyatt Wingfoot began to intercede and were arrested. A vicious crowd sprang up and started to hurl bricks at the FF. While Reed and Johnny attempted to find the source of the hostility, Sue escorted Alicia home. Hatred was in the air....

A MOMENT OF YOUR TIME, SHE-HULK.

THERE IS AN *ORDEAL* THROUGH WHICH YOU MUST PASS BEFORE YOU GO ANY FURTHER.

IF YOU GO ANY FUR-THER, AFTER YOUR *ULTIMATE DEFEAT* AT THE HANDS OF **MALICE, MISTRESS OF HATE!**

YOU HAVE GOT TO BE *KIDDING!*

Malice was secretly being controlled by the new Hate Monger, who wanted to fan the flames of class, racial, and religious bigotry into a violent street war.

?!?

YOU'RE STILL *STANDING?!* BUT THAT *PUNCH* WOULD HAVE STOPPED A CHARGING *RHINO!*

THEN I SUGGEST YOU *SAVE* IT FOR THE OCCASION WHEN YOU FIND YOURSELF FAC-ING SUCH A BEAST.

FOR IT WILL SERVE YOU *NAUGHT* AGAINST ME!

Savaging the She-Hulk

The police van carrying Wyatt and the She-Hulk was attacked sometime later. While Wyatt helped the injured, a costumed woman named Malice appeared. She caused the ground beneath the She-Hulk to rise in the air and sent her crashing into the Earth. She-Hulk's strongest blows could not harm Malice. As Malice floated above, She-Hulk found that she could not breathe and lost consciousness—Malice had cut off her air supply. Moments later, Malice revealed her real identity—Susan Richards, the Invisible Girl!

With Malice toward all

Reed discovered that the Hate Monger had distributed pamphlets across the city. Each one contained an alien hypno-poison that drove people into uncontrollable rages. Reed created a device to counteract the poison but was attacked by Malice. He quickly recognized his disguised wife. Believing that Sue's emotions were being altered by the Hate Monger, Reed reasoned that he could free her by making her angry at him. His plan worked, and Sue revealed that the Psycho-Man was secretly behind the Hate Monger.

YOU SEE, FOOL? YOU SEE HOW *EASY* IT IS FOR *MALICE* TO *DESTROY* YOU?

ONLY... BECAUSE I HAD NOT ANTICIPATED THE FULL EXTENT OF YOUR POWERS.

BUT I HAPPEN TO BE A SCIENTIST. I ALWAYS *LEARN* FROM MY MISTAKES.

YOU'LL NOT TAKE ME OFF-GUARD A SECOND TIME!

YOU TOOK *MUCH* LONGER TO FIGURE IT OUT THAN I'D EXPECTED, MY "LOVED ONES."

MY LOVING *HUSBAND.* MY DEVOTED *BROTHER.*

BUT THEN, WHY WOULD YOU EVEN *CONSIDER* THAT YOUR UTTER DEFEAT COULD COME AT THE HANDS OF ONE FOR WHOM YOU HAVE *NO RESPECT...* SUSAN STORM... THE INVISIBLE GIRL!!!

OPPOSITES ATTACK

Malice's emotions were the complete opposite of Sue's. Sue's strongest feelings were love and compassion; Malice's were hatred and cruelty. While their powers were the same, Malice used her invisible force fields without restraint and reveled in ferocity. Malice would not hesitate to use invisible sharp-bladed objects or force-bubbles that deprived her enemies of oxygen.

Hate Monger

The original Hate Monger was a clone who believed that he was a member of a master race that would rule the world. He used a "hate-ray," which magnified his victim's feelings of fear and anger. While battling the FF, he fired at two of his underlings, who then killed him. Aware of the first Hate Monger, Psycho-Man built an android that could change its sex, race, or appearance. The new Hate Monger preached bigotry and violence. It used the Psycho-Man's emotion-controlling technology to induce irrational hatred. The android also distributed Psycho-Man's chemical-coated pamphlets. Assuming Reed's appearance, the Hate Monger brainwashed Sue and transformed her into Malice.

The girl becomes a woman

After journeying to the microverse home of Psycho-Man and enacting her revenge, Sue began to reevaluate herself and her powers. She decided that the time had finally come for her to change her name from the Invisible Girl to the Invisible Woman. Unfortunately, Sue had not seen the last of Malice. Malice's evil persona continued to lurk deep within Sue's subconscious, looking for a way to escape. Sue eventually tried to integrate Malice into her conscious mind. Still not content, Malice jumped into the mind of the teenage Franklin from an alternate timeline was eventually destroyed.

IT ISN'T ENOUGH!

YOU AND THE OTHERS WILL NEVER SURVIVE WITHOUT MY *NAKED* AGGRESSION!

I AM HURLING RAZOR-SHARP INVISI-BLADES RIGHT AT YOU, MY DEAR--

UNLEASH THE TRUE SUSAN RICHARDS!

THROW OFF YOUR INHIBITIONS, YOUR PSYCHOLOGICAL RESTRAINTS!!!

FREE THE SHE-DEVIL THAT LIES WITHIN!

Malice tried to encourage Sue to embrace and free her inner she-devil.

ACCEPT THE FACT THAT YOU'VE ALWAYS BEEN THE MOST POWERFUL, DEADLIEST MEMBER OF THE *FANTASTIC FOUR--*

--AND REVEL IN UNRESTRAINED *FEROCITY!*

Though the Psycho-Man released her evil persona, Sue secretly feared that Malice was actually the result of unresolved anger over the death of Sue's mother and imprisonment of her father.

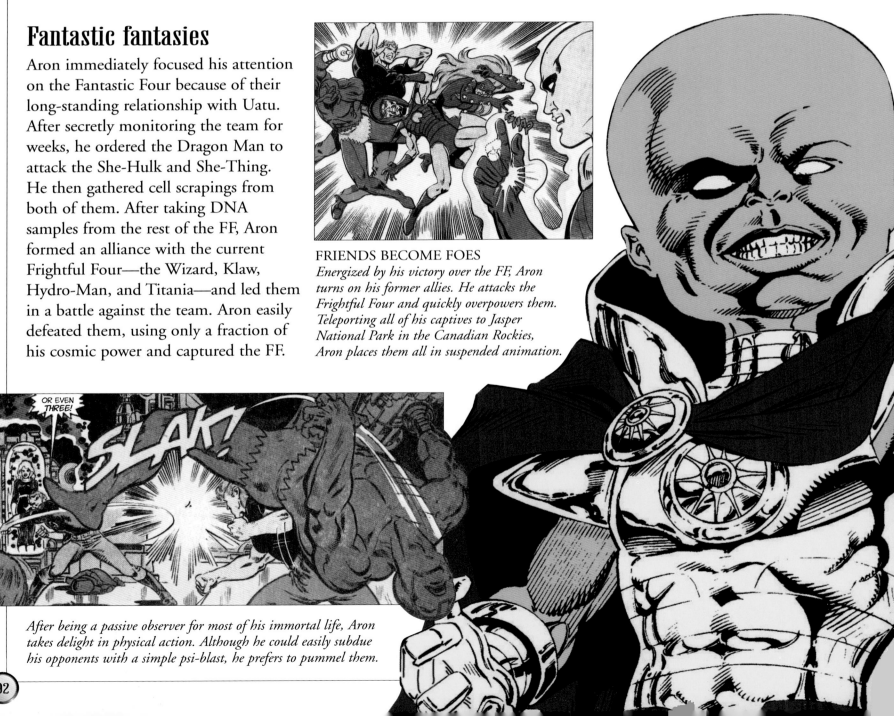

ARON THE WATCHER AND DRAGON MAN WOULD LOVE TO DESTROY THE FANTASTIC FOUR!

Aron secures the services of the Dragon Man as his agent on Earth to try to conceal his involvement from Uatu.

Aron The renegade Watcher

A MEMBER OF the alien race known as the Watchers, Aron became curious about the Earth when he learned that Uatu had occasionally violated his sacred oath to help the planet's inhabitants. After observing countless worlds for untold millennia, Aron had grown bored. He was tired of watching and wanted to use his vast powers proactively. Cloaking himself so that Uatu could not perceive him, Aron journeyed to Earth and took up residence in an office on the 100th floor of the Empire State Building. He began to observe humanity and immediately became intoxicated with their active lives and imaginations.

Fantastic fantasies

Aron immediately focused his attention on the Fantastic Four because of their long-standing relationship with Uatu. After secretly monitoring the team for weeks, he ordered the Dragon Man to attack the She-Hulk and She-Thing. He then gathered cell scrapings from both of them. After taking DNA samples from the rest of the FF, Aron formed an alliance with the current Frightful Four—the Wizard, Klaw, Hydro-Man, and Titania—and led them in a battle against the team. Aron easily defeated them, using only a fraction of his cosmic power and captured the FF.

FRIENDS BECOME FOES
Energized by his victory over the FF, Aron turns on his former allies. He attacks the Frightful Four and quickly overpowers them. Teleporting all of his captives to Jasper National Park in the Canadian Rockies, Aron places them all in suspended animation.

OR EVEN THREE!

SLAK!

After being a passive observer for most of his immortal life, Aron takes delight in physical action. Although he could easily subdue his opponents with a simple psi-blast, he prefers to pummel them.

The Dreamquest Saga

With the real Fantastic Four out of the way, Aron constructed clones out of their DNA. These doubles followed Aron's mental commands, enabling him to live out his fantasies by proxy. The public soon noticed a difference in the team. The clones were nastier and far more aggressive than the real FF. When the Avengers investigated the doppelgängers, a battle erupted, and the real FF finally freed themselves. Realizing that his doubles would allow him to fulfill plenty of his fantasies, Aron fled with them.

--SO I'VE CREATED A SET OF PAWNS!

Dreams and schemes

Aron soon tired of his doubles and exiled them to an alternate dimension. He returned to Earth and kidnapped Alicia Masters because he found her personal fantasies much more tantalizing than mere reality. Desperate to rescue his step-daughter, the Puppet Master forced the Molecule Man to go after her. Doctor Doom joined the battle and temporarily stole Aron's cosmic power. After Aron regained his power, the other Watchers put him on trial for his crimes against humanity. He managed to escape into an alternate dimension when they became embroiled in a war with another alien race.

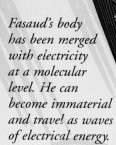

Fasaud's body has been merged with electricity at a molecular level. He can become immaterial and travel as waves of electrical energy.

Fasaud

Sheikh Farouk al-Fasaud was one of the wealthiest and most influential businessmen in the world until a reporter exposed his unscrupulous tactics. Furious, the sheikh cornered the reporter in a television studio and attempted to kill him. A freak electrical accident drew all the power in the studio into the sheikh's body and transformed him into a living television image. The Fantastic Four clashed with Fasaud when he came to New York to try to murder the reporter again. Fasaud defeated the Thing and Ms. Marvel, who learned that the former sheikh was using a communications satellite to transmit himself around the world. The Thing borrowed a space shuttle and destroyed the satellite while Fasaud was in mid-transmission. His fate is still unknown.

FINAL BATTLE

While hopping between dimensions, Aron meets an alternate version of Reed Richards who is consumed by madness because he failed to save his world from Galactus. They team up and try to eliminate all the other versions of Reed in the multiverse. The FF stop the dark Reed, but Aron escapes to a secret base in the asteroid belt. He creates a device to convert the entire Milky Way into his own personal mini universe, but the FF destroy it. As Aron prepares to obliterate them, Uatu arrives and saves his friends from the rogue Watcher.

NO, ARON! THE MADNESS ENDS HERE --AND NOW!

STAND ASIDE! SURRENDER! I HAVE NO WISH TO HARM YOU!

I DO NOT FEAR YOU, UATU! THOUGH YOU HAVE OCCASIONALLY DISREGARDED YOUR SACRED OATH-- --YOU WILL NOT ENGAGE ME IN MORTAL COMBAT!

YOUR DEVOTION TO HUMANKIND HAS ALWAYS BEEN YOUR MOST EXPLOITABLE WEAKNESS, UATU!

WHY DO YOU CARE ABOUT THESE PUNY INSECTS? WHY?!

Beyonder aka Kosmos

AN IMMENSELY powerful entity from a dimension outside our universe, the Beyonder was brought into being by the nuclear accident that transformed Owen Reece into the Molecule Man. He observed the Earth for many years through a rift between his dimension (known as the Beyond-Realm) and our own and became fascinated by the desires of individual, sentient human beings. In his own realm, he himself was the sum total of all creation. To satisfy his curiosity, he ensnared the world's greatest heroes and their adversaries, including the Fantastic Four and Doctor Doom, and transported them to his dimension.

HUMAN FORM
When the Beyonder assumed human form, he often appeared as a tall, dark-haired male.

Birth of a planet

Lured into a mysterious alien construct that had appeared in New York City's Central Park, the FF and their heroic allies were instantly transported into the Beyond-Realm. On arrival, they found themselves in deep space. Protected inside the force-shielded construct, they watched in amazement as Beyonder annihilated an entire galaxy around them, except for a single star. He then created a new planet near the star. To satisfy the Beyonder's fascination with human nature, his captives were later forced to engage in a "secret war" on the planet, which was named Battleworld.

WE'RE MOVING--! AT FANTASTIC SPEED!

UP AHEAD! A-- A PLANET IS BEING FORMED NEAR THAT STAR--!

THE ONLY STAR REMAINING FROM THAT ENTIRE GALAXY!

AWE-INSPIRING... HUMBLING ...FEATS DWARFING THE WILDEST IMAGININGS OF THE GODS!

THE POWER NECESSARY... IT'S INCALCU-LABLE... IN-CONCEIVABLE!

OAF! WATCH WHO YOU'RE JOSTLING, OR, I, *DOCTOR OCTOPUS,* WILL--

HEY, I'M *SORRY,* BUTT-HEAD! I, CRUSHER CREEL, THE *ABSORBIN' MAN* WUZ WATCHIN' THE SHOW OUTSIDE! THAT'S KEEPIN' ME REAL BUSY RIGHT NOW, BUT WHEN IT'S DONE I'LL RAM YOU THROUGH A BULKHEAD SO'S YOU AND YOUR STUPID TENTACLES WON'T BE UNDERFOOT NO MORE!

AWESOME ABILITIES
A second construct carried Doctor Doom and other criminals, such as the Absorbing Man and Doctor Octopus into the Beyonder's dimension. Although a scientific genius himself, Doom was awestruck by the entity's power.

Doom's new powers

Motivated by Beyonder's promise of a valuable prize, the criminals battled the FF and their allies (including the Avengers and the X-Men). Doom used his technological abilities to steal some of the Beyonder's incredible powers but found them difficult to control. Weakened, the Beyonder eventually reclaimed his abilities and returned the warring participants to their own dimension.

THIS IS GOING TO BE THE FIGHT OF OUR LIVES!

ON MY COMMAND, ATTACK! AND DON'T STOP... DON'T LET UP...NO MATTER WHAT!

WE MUST FIND A WAY..., WE *WILL* FIND A WAY TO WIN!

READY...!

GOOD LORD! HE'S-- THE SUN!

YOU'RE ALL *DEAD!*

OMNIPOTENT ENTITY

In his dimension, the Beyonder was himself the entire reality. He was literally the sun, the stars, and the planets and could appear in any form he chose.

Return to the Beyond-Realm

In a later encounter with the Human Torch, the Thing, Ms. Marvel, the Molecule Man, and Doctor Doom, the Beyonder appeared both as a flaming sun and in human form. Angry at their intrusion into his realm, he threatened to destroy them. Before he could do so, the cosmic intelligence Kubik appeared and engaged him in battle. Determined to show the Beyonder the error of his aggressive ways, Kubik destroyed most of the Beyonder's reality. Kubik was about to destroy the entity when the alien Shaper of Worlds stopped the battle. Under the Shaper's guidance, Kubik, Molecule Man, and the Beyonder realized they shared a common origin. Combining their life forces, the Molecule Man and Beyonder became a cosmic cube, which ultimately evolved into the being known as Kosmos.

WE HAVE WATCHED YOU FROM *AFAR,* BEYONDER

THAT'S *NONSENSE!* I WOULD HAVE *KNOWN!*

NO-- YOU WOULD *NOT!*

BELIEVE ME, CREATURE... I *WOULD!*

WE HAVE WATCHED YOU FROM *AFAR,* BEYONDER, AND WE SAW THE *ERROR* TAKE ROOT IN YOUR MIND!

YOU CALL ALL *THIS* AN ERROR?

I *DON'T ERR!*

EVOLUTION

A fusion of the Molecule Man and the Beyonder, Kosmos took on female form. She did so because she believed the psychological flaws of her previous incarnations were linked to aggressive male characteristics.

CUBE'S CREATION

Like Kosmos, Kubik previously existed as a cosmic cube. Imbued with almost limitless energies, these cubes can alter reality and create new life forms. In a nuclear accident, laboratory worker Owen Reece released extra-dimensional energy, mutating him into the Molecule Man. This also created a portal into the Beyond-Realm, into which some of the energy escaped. This energy developed into the intelligence known as the Beyonder. When Molecule Man and the Beyonder merged to become a new cosmic cube, the two products of the nuclear accident were reunited to create Kosmos.

ROCKY GRIMM AND TARIANNA.

GETTING KINDA COLD DON'TCHA THINK, TARI?

YES, BENGRIMM, THERE IS A CHILL IN THE AIR TONIGHT.

Rocky Grimm

After the "secret war" conflicts on Battleworld, the Thing remained there for a time when the other heroes and criminals were returned to Earth. There, Ben was able to change form at will, choosing to lead an alternate life in his unmutated form. Adopting the nickname Rocky, Ben explored the planet, becoming involved in numerous adventures as a "Space Ranger." He became close to a woman called Tarianna, a warrior of the Leenin people, and her family. The sensitivity of Battleworld to human desires eventually led the two sides of Ben to split, and he literally battled himself. The human Ben wanted to kill the mutated Thing-side of his identity, but in succeeding, he lost his own humanity. As a result, he was transformed back into the Thing— this time for good. His anger over this, Tarianna's tragic death, and other old scores led to the Thing taking on the Beyonder in an epic wrestling match.

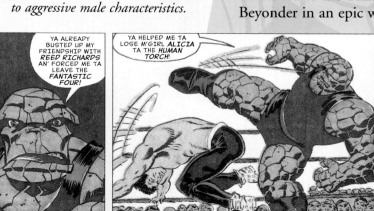

YA ALREADY BUSTED UP MY FRIENDSHIP WITH *REED RICHARDS* AN' FORCED ME TA LEAVE THE *FANTASTIC FOUR!*

YA HELPED ME TA LOSE M'GIRL *ALICIA* TA THE *HUMAN TORCH!*

AN' YER ROTTEN *SECRET WARS* PLANET MADE ME DESTROY MY HUMAN-SELF *FOREVER!*

THOSE ARE JUST A *FEW* OF YER HIT PARADE, PAL... THE REASONS I WANT YER HIDE, BEYONDER, AN' I AM GONNA HAVE IT!!!

The Fantastic Four in the 1990s

Writer and artist Walt Simonson jump-started the new decade by taking the Fantastic Four into the time-stream in which they visited an alternate Earth on the verge of World War III and ran into dinosaurs on an island that time forgot! After curing Sharon Ventura of her plight as the She-Thing and making Ben Grimm the Thing again, Walt resolved the war between Kristoff and Doctor Doom. He also sent the FF on a wild ride on the Cross-Time Express. A childhood dream came true for Tom DeFalco when, along with artist Paul Ryan, he got a shot at the World's Greatest Comic Magazine. We started with a war with the New Warriors, then revealed that Johnny had married a Skrull, and introduced new villains like Paibok, Devos, and Occulus. We explored new realities like the Inniverse, gave Sue a new outfit, had Wolverine scar the Thing's face, and transformed Franklin into a teenager. The FF suffered a devastating loss when Reed Richards and Doom were apparently killed. The Ant-Man and Kristoff temporarily joined the team in time to discover that Watchers lie, and Atlantis rose from the sea. After Reed and Doom returned, Marvel canceled the long-running series and hired superstar writer/artist Jim Lee to recreate the FF with a new origin and new backgrounds for the characters. It was later decided that Jim's stories occurred in a pocket universe and Scott Lobdell and Alan Davis brought back the real FF. Lobdell and Davis were followed by writer Chris Claremont and artist Salvador Larroca.

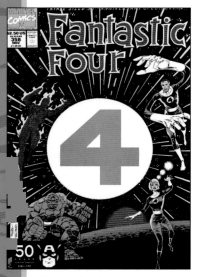

Fantastic Four #358
(Nov. 1991) 30th anniversary
die-cut cover. (Cover by Paul Ryan
and Danny Bulanadi)

Fantastic Four Unlimited #1 (Mar. 1993)
*Roy Thomas returns to the FF in a new series
drawn by legendary artist Herb Trimpe.
(Cover by Mark Pacella and Brad Vancata)*

1990

Fantastic Four #337 (Feb. 1990).
*The FF head into the time-stream
with Thor and Iron Man.
(Cover by Walt Simonson)*

1991

Fantastic Four #350 (March 1991).
*The real Thing and Dr. Doom return to
commemorate the FF's 350th issue!
(Cover by Walt Simonson)*

1992

Fantastic Four #368 (Sept. 1992).
*The FF fight evil versions of the X-Men.
(Cover by Paul Ryan and Danny
Bulanadi)*

1993

Fantastic Four #381 (Nov. 1993).
*Believing that he is soon to die, Dr. Doom
takes revenge on Reed. (Cover by Paul Ryan
and Danny Bulanadi)*

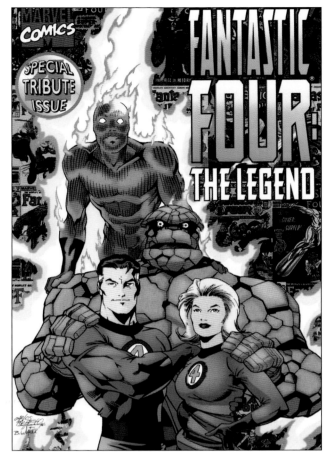

Fantastic Four: The Legend *(Oct. 1996). As the first volume ends with* Fantastic Four #416, *Marvel Comics honors the world's greatest comic with a special tribute issue. (Cover by Carlos Pacheco and Bob Wiacek)*

Fantastic Four #400 *(May 1995).*
With Reed still presumed dead, the new team gets caught in the middle of a war between the Watchers and the Celestials. Marvel celebrates 400 issues with a holographic cover. (Cover by Paul Ryan and Danny Bulanadi)

1994

Fantastic Four #387 *(April 1994). The FF are warned that no one will survive the next mission. (Cover by Paul Ryan and Danny Bulanadi)*

1995

Fantastic Four #405 *(Oct. 1995). While hunting for Reed, the FF confront an army of old foes. (Cover by Paul Ryan and Danny Bulanadi)*

1998

Fantastic Four *Vol. 3 #1 (Jan. 1998). Scott Lobdell and Alan Davis return the FF to the real Marvel Universe. (Cover by Alan Davis and Mark Farmer)*

1999

Fantastic Four *Vol. 3 #19 (July 1999). The FF runs into Annihilus while in the Negative Zone. (Cover by Salvador Larroca and Art Thibert)*

All New Fantastic Four

INSIDE THE ORBIT of the moon, a spacecraft phased out of subspace and entered our plane of reality. Severely damaged, the ship headed for the Earth, crashing moments later and marooning its sole occupant. Hours later a beautiful woman entered Four Freedoms Plaza and asked to see the Fantastic Four. After being told that the FF would not see her without an appointment, she apparently disappeared. However, a few minutes later, familiar faces appeared to the individual members of the FF and shocked each one into unconsciousness. Meanwhile, out beyond the orbit of Mars, a Skrull battleship phased into our solar system. The Skrulls were on the trail of De'Lila, a traitor to their empire. They scanned for Skrull mind-waves and detected them on an island in the Bermuda Triangle called Monster Isle.

SURPRISE!
With shape-shifting abilities, De'Lila tricks each FF member by appearing to be someone they trust before stunning them with a synapse disrupter.

Big trouble on little Earth

Suspecting that the Skrull Empire was after her, De'Lila secured the FF and sent out a call for help. Spider-Man, the Hulk, Wolverine, and Ghost Rider responded. Disguised as Sue, De'Lila told them that assassins had murdered the other members of the FF and were planning to kill more people. She gave them a tracking device and sent them after the supposed killers.

Where monsters dwell

On Monster Isle, the Skrulls discovered giant creatures. Deciding to use them to find De'Lila, the aliens targeted them with slave darts and scattered them around the world. The Mole Man ruled Monster Isle and got angry when he learned that Skrulls were using his monsters. He captured the aliens and threatened to kill them unless they returned his creatures. As the Skrulls obeyed, the All New FF arrived on Monster Isle and prepared to avenge the old FF.

Mind games

At Four Freedoms Plaza, De'Lila freed Reed and controlled him with telepathy. She needed his help to find an inorganic technotroid that could hide itself until ready to hatch. Believing his friends would free themselves, Reed bought time by pretending to be in love with De'Lila. He tracked the technotroid to a cave in an underground network that led to Monster Isle.

AN EGG, RICHARDS. AN EGG SUCH AS YOU HAVE NEVER *DREAMED* OF! WE'RE LOOKING FOR AN *INORGANIC TECHNOTROID*, AN *ITT!*

IN ITS DORMANT STATE, AN ITT IS A SPHERE... BUT IT'S SELF-PROPELLED...

...CAPABLE OF CONCEALING ITSELF UNTIL IT'S READY TO HATCH! AND IT CAN DEFEND ITSELF IF NECESSARY.

IT'S *OUT* THERE SOME-WHERE, RICHARDS, HIDING, BUT IT MUST HAVE BEEN *SEEN* AT SOME POINT!

SOME-WHERE, IN THE VOLUMINOUS RECORDS OF YOUR SOCIETY IS THE ANSWER. AND I *WANT* IT!

Dangerous, deceitful De'Lila

De'Lila is a mutant Skrull, who is both a telepath and an empath. Not only can she read minds, but she can also sense emotions and use them to her advantage by convincing her victims that they love her. She wanted the technotroid because it was indestructible and the perfect assassin to use to slay the Skrull Emperor.

IT'S *TRUE!* I'M *NOT* SUSAN RICHARDS; I *AM* A SKRULL!

STAY WHERE YOU ARE! WHAT'S THE *MEANING* OF THIS *INTRUSION?*

IT FIGURES! THAT'S *GOTTA* BE THE *MOLE MAN!* AND HIS JOLLY CREW!

IF THAT OVERSIZED *TOMATO PLANT* IS ONE OF *YOURS,* PEE WEE, THEN YOU'RE *JUST* THE GUY I WANT TO SEE!

Eggs got legs

The technotroid would become enslaved to the first living thing it saw, so even the Mole Man joined the race to find it. However, when it hatched, the robot bonded with one of the Mole Man's giant monsters. The original FF was reunited, and De'Lila was turned over to the Skrulls.

THE ALL NEW FF
The temporary new Fantastic Four consists of a friendly neighborhood web-swinger, a mutant berserker, a bad-tempered monster, and the living spirit of vengeance.

THE NOSE SEEMS A LITTLE OFF!

OTHERWISE... PERFECT!

Lyja

AN INTELLIGENCE officer for the Skrull military, Lyja infiltrated the Fantastic Four in the guise of Alicia Masters, the Thing's blind girlfriend. Using her Skrull shape-changing abilities to match the real Alicia's appearance, Lyja successfully duped the team for a considerable amount of time. Her deception was exposed when the Puppet Master revealed her true identity to Ben Grimm. By this time, Lyja had fallen in love with Johnny Storm and was ready to help the FF rescue the real Alicia Masters from the Skrulls' clutches.

Skrull spy

In order to be convincing in her assumed guise, Lyja absorbed every piece of information in the Skrull archives about the FF, Alicia Masters, and the planet Earth. She also had to learn to function as a blind person,

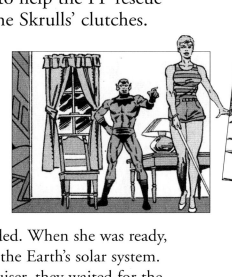

including being able to walk unaided. When she was ready, Lyja and a Skrull team traveled to the Earth's solar system. Orbiting the Moon in a stealth cruiser, they waited for the chance to substitute Lyja for the real Alicia.

Kidnap attempt

When Reed Richards, Ben Grimm, and Johnny Storm were unexpectedly transported to the Beyond-Realm, the Skrulls made their move, abducting Alicia. Lyja then befriended Sue Storm, establishing herself with ease. But when Reed and Johnny returned without Alicia's boyfriend, Ben, Lyja changed her plan and decided to focus her attention on Johnny.

SKRULL SCHEME
The Skrulls abduct the real Alicia Masters, taking her to the War World.

BLIND EYES
As the final touch in her deception, Lyja is surgically fitted with special contact lenses that render her blind while in human form.

"THAT'S WHEN I LEARNED THE TERRIBLE TRUTH--!"

ALICIA, I-I'D GIVE ANYTHING NOT TO HAVE TO TELL YOU THIS... BUT BEN... WELL, HE... HE ISN'T... HE *WON'T* BE COMING BACK!

THE SHE-HULK HAS TEMPORARILY REPLACED HIM!

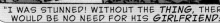
"I WAS STUNNED! WITHOUT THE *THING*, THERE WOULD BE NO NEED FOR HIS *GIRLFRIEND!*"

Lyja revealed

With Ben Grimm replaced by the She-Hulk during the Thing's stay in the Beyond-Realm, the duplicitous relationship between Johnny and Lyja blossomed into marriage. When Ben returned to Earth, he was upset at first but soon accepted the situation. Happy in his relationship, Johnny was devastated when Ben burst into their apartment on discovering the true identity of "Alicia." Repentant, Lyja offered to help rescue the real Alicia in return for her freedom. Dressed in Sue Storm's original FF uniform to distinguish her from other Skrulls, Lyja led the team to the Skrull War World. Although the FF succeeded in their mercy mission, Lyja sacrificed herself to save Johnny, dying in his arms.

Lyja the Lazer-fist

After her apparent death on the War World, Lyja was revived by Paibok, the Power Skrull, and, months later, returned to Earth. Angry at the Human Torch for "abandoning" her and their unborn child, they engaged in battle at Empire State University. Able to shoot energy blasts from her hands after being genetically engineered by Paibok, she now called herself Lyja the Lazer-fist. Eventually their conflict was resolved, and Johnny and his estranged wife rekindled their relationship during a desperate battle against Onslaught.

Paibok

A bionically re-engineered Skrull military officer, Paibok was responsible for planning Lyja's original infiltration mission. Naming himself the Power Skrull, Paibok has superhuman strength and the ability to fly. His skin is as strong as steel, and he can project blasts of electricity and ice. Paibok was instrumental in resuscitating and transforming Lyja after the Fantastic Four's assault on War World. When he later became an outcast from the Skrull empire, he sought out scientists to further enhance his powers, but his appearance became that of a living corpse.

SKRULL POWER
Paibok's abilities nearly enable him to defeat the FF in their first encounter.

Devos The Devastator

ORPHANED ON a distant alien world, Devos was enrolled in the army, where he quickly became a great warrior. Scientist Symka saw potential in him and chose him to take part in the "Great Experiment," which altered his genetic structure and granted him astonishing power. Devos decided he would use this power to bring peace by destroying any race capable of war, believing this was his sacred responsibility. Following this principle through to its logical conclusion means that the "guardian of galactic peace" is paradoxically determined to destroy every race!

Evil eliminator

Finding the Fantastic Four's ship, Devos captured the team and brought them onto his Death Cruiser. Seeing a threat in the human race, Devos confronted the FF and used up vast amounts of energy in trying to destroy the Thing. Mr. Fantastic was able to knock the weakened Devos into the energy grid, causing the Cruiser to self-destruct. However, Devos escaped just in time.

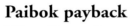

Paibok payback

When Devos first met the Power-Skrull Paibok, he thought he had a fight on his hands. However, the pair realized that they shared a common enemy—the FF. Joined by Klaw and Huntara and given the moniker the Fearsome Foursome, the group captured the Fantastic Four and presented them to the Skrull Empire at their new Throneworld. Paibok found out that Devos was wanted by the Skrulls and tried to arrest him. A fight ensued, resulting in Devos taking his Death Cruiser into battle. Unbeknown to him, Paibok had climbed on board, sabotaged the ship, and sent it into sub-space. Devos was later seen at a meeting for enemies of the FF.

Initially, Paibok and Devos were united against the Fantastic Four. This soon changed when Paibok realized that Devos planned to destroy the Skrulls—and that there was a substantial price on the devastator's head.

WAR AND PEACE

Measuring over seven feet tall, Devos is one of the great warriors. The key to Devos's power lies within his armor. The suit houses twin blades, electric blasts, knock-out gas, infra-red detectors, miniature missiles, and the Luminator, which can blind opponents. His armor is also the reason for his superhuman strength and ability to fly.

Occulus Power Incarnate

IN AN ALTERNATE dimension called the Inniverse, an Earthlike universe that can be accessed by entering the space between atomic and sub-atomic particles, a young Occulus and his brother Wildblood were tested by the Gem Guild to detect if they could manipulate the energy in the power gems that orbited their world. Occulus was blessed with this power and was taken by the Gem Guild. No one knows why he later plucked out his right eye and replaced it with a power gem. Was it madness or a ploy to gain greater personal power? Either way, Occulus's power grew until he ruled the Gem Guild and the entire Inniverse.

Brotherly love

Hearing that Wildblood opposed the Gem Guild, Occulus sent his army to capture his brother. They found that Wildblood had escaped to Earth through a portal constructed by Reed. They fought the Fantastic Four and brought Wildblood, Sue, and Franklin to the Inniverse. While Ben, Reed, and Johnny tried to rescue the others, Occulus discovered that Franklin's psionic powers were connected to the powers of the gems. His instinct was to kill Franklin but he decided instead to harness Franklin's powers to magnify his own.

Power-hungry

Occulus found that he could now command all the gems that fill the Inniverse skies. He let the FF free Sue and Franklin but then confronted the rest of the group. The battle that ensued saw Reed use his Enervator, a device that saps gem power, on Occulus, weakening his power. Under Reed's instruction, the Rebel Underground—the Gem Guild's enemy—built a screen that could attack Occulus's energies, sending the bejeweled one into space. He reappeared at the meeting for FF enemies.

OMNIPOTENCE
The all-seeing Occulus wants more than blind obedience from the inhabitants of the Inniverse. However, Occulus's people fear their leader and his ever-consuming power.

Nobody Gets Out Alive

EVEN THOUGH she had watched as Reed Richards and Doctor Doom were disintegrated, Sue Richards refused to believe her husband was dead. She knew that Doom could have faked their deaths and taken them to a hidden lair—especially since the newspapers were printing recent photos of Doom! After seizing Doom's matter-transference computer from his castle in Latveria, Sue asked her science consultant Scott (Ant-Man) Lang to link it to their space/time sled so that the Fantastic Four could teleport to Doom's receiving stations and secret hiding places.

Terrible tidings

While Sue made the preparations for her search, an apparition appeared before the Fantastic Four. Engulfed in flames, an image of a younger Sue in one of her old costumes said she had witnessed the deaths of Ben and Johnny. Within minutes, the team also learned that Franklin had hijacked their space/time-sled. Fearing the prophecy, the team debated its course of action, but Sue knew what she must do.

At the mercy of Malice

Sue never fully accepted Franklin as a teenager. However, he learned that Sue was being manipulated by Malice and tried to rescue her. Malice mind-leaped into his subconscious and influenced him. Sue did not care what the others decided. She was going after her son.

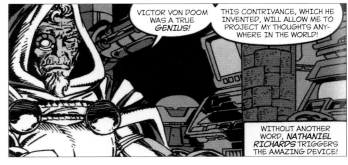

The new Doom

Unbeknown to the FF, Nathaniel Richards had gone to Latveria and taken control of Castle Doom, masquerading as the missing ruler. Still claiming that the universe was in danger from an unrevealed enemy, Nathaniel contacted Franklin and hinted that Reed was alive. Desperate to find Reed and enlist his aid, the teen sneaked into FF headquarters, assaulted Lang, and stole the space/time sled.

INTO THE TIME-STREAM

Scott has linked the space/time sled to the FF's old time platform so that they can track Franklin through time and space. Scott feels responsible for the loss of the sled, so he joins Sue, Ben, and Johnny, who plan to defy the prophecy.

Back from the dead

Using their time platform the team materialized in the original Baxter Building. Wondering why Franklin had led them there, they entered a nearby laboratory. Unable to believe her eyes, Sue recognized the man standing before her. He was her missing husband!

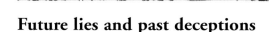

Deadly is the Dark Raider

Unfortunately, Sue quickly realized that this was a Reed from an earlier time period and met younger versions of Johnny, Ben, and herself. As the two teams eyed each other suspiciously, Franklin appeared on the scene. Goaded by Malice, he sparked a fight between the different groups. During the course of the battle, a mysterious figure suddenly materialized. Calling himself the Dark Raider, he murdered the younger Reed and Sue and revealed that his mission was to destroy every possible version of Reed Richards. Believing that he had finally met Nathaniel's great enemy, Franklin slipped away from the others and started hunting the Dark Raider.

Future lies and past deceptions

Leaping from one alternate reality to the next, the Fantastic Four were always one step behind the Dark Raider, who left a trail of dead Reeds in his wake. The FF arrived in a distant future, where they learned that New York had been destroyed, and they were responsible.

They moved backward through that timeline, turning up just as their younger selves faced a battle with Galactus. Reed was sent to retrieve the Ultimate Nullifier but did not return in time. The prophecy came true when Galactus incinerated Ben and Johnny before consuming the Earth.

The Raider revealed

After watching their counterparts die, the FF returned to their own reality. They were soon attacked by the Dark Raider, who revealed that he was the Reed who failed to save his world. As the team was joined by the Watcher and Franklin, the Raider attempted to activate the Ultimate Nullifier and erase the entire universe.

O' bitter victory

After centuries of inaction, the Watcher obliterated the Dark Raider before he had time to carry out his threat. The Watcher then had to go into exile for violating his sacred oath. Still believing that her Reed was alive, Sue quit the Fantastic Four so that she could devote all her time to finding her missing husband.

Fantastic Force

AFTER LEARNING that one of his subjects was a teenage mutant, the Black Panther met a young Inhuman who was having problems with his new powers. T'Challa took the pair to the Fantastic Four, where they met Franklin Richards (Psi-Lord) and Huntara. When Sue Richards quit the FF, the four teens formed a super-team.

THRUKK!

"HOW DID YOU EVER COPE WITH A CHILD OF SUCH VAST DESTRUCTIVE POTENTIAL?"

I...I DOUBT I'M READY FOR A FIGHT LIKE THIS...BUT I AIN'T GOT MUCH CHOICE!

Huntara

The daughter of Nathaniel Richards, Huntara grew up in a barbaric alien dimension, where she was trained in the arts of war and personal combat. Her weapon of choice is a psionic scythe that can cut through almost any material known to man, can fire deadly concussive blasts, and allows her to teleport herself.

Legacy

Aside from the teenage Franklin Richards (who possessed telekinetic and telepathic powers) and Huntara, the Fantastic Force had two other members. Vibraxas was a haughty Wakandan, able to generate and direct powerful vibrations in any object that he touched. Devlor the deadly was a short and insecure Inhuman who could transform into a giant-sized, super-strong creature.

From the ashes

Funded by the Black Panther, the Fantastic Force was almost a reverse image of the FF. The original team was a normal family that explored the extraordinary world; the new team was an extraordinary family that explored the normal world. They battled Klaw, rogue Inhumans, the Puppet Master, and Diablo. The new team's ranks swelled to include T'Challa, the Human Torch, and She-Hulk.

A FORCE OF ONE

The team ultimately disbands after they learn that Reed Richards is still alive. Franklin goes on to rejoin his parents.

Hyperstorm

IN A POSSIBLE future that may never occur, Franklin Richards grew to manhood in a concentration camp for mutants and married Rachel Summers. Rachel had the powers of Phoenix, a near-infinite force that came from the psionic energies of all living beings. Their only son became Hyperstorm, the most powerful mutant ever, and lashed out at the world that enslaved his parents.

NO HUMAN BEING HAS EVER *POSSESSED* THE POWER WHICH IS *MINE!* I TRULY CONTROL THE *POWER SUPREME!*

ON YOUR *KNEES*, YOU HELPLESS SIMPLETONS! YOUR *SALVATION* TEETERS ON MY WHIM! *GET ON YOUR KNEES--!*

ALL TIMES & SPACE
Since he is already the absolute master of his particular universe, Hyperstorm plans to extend his empire to include every time period and alternate dimension.

The great enemy

After conquering the Earth, Hyperstorm extended his empire to include the rest of the known universe. While studying possible timelines, Franklin's grandfather, Nathaniel, learned about his great-grandson and tried to stop his rise to power. Nathaniel kidnapped Franklin as a child and returned him as a teenager. Hyperstorm snatched Reed and Doctor Doom from the present and convinced the world that they were dead.

YOU *KIDNAPPED* ME, AND EXILED ME TO THE DISTANT PAST!

AND NOW YOU DARE *ATTACK* THE WOMAN I LOVE!

Strange days

Searching for Reed, Sue found Hyperstorm's timeline and learned that Reed had been exiled to an ancient Earth. Reunited, the FF battled Hyperstorm but could not defeat him. Though he could have killed them, Hyperstorm zapped the FF back to their own time.

I AM GALACTUS! MY GNAWING HUNGER CAN NO LONGER BE DENIED!

THUS, I MUST FEAST UPON THE *LIVING ENERGIES* WHICH I SENSE WITHIN YOU!

The forever war

Determined to save the multiverse, Reed lured Hyperstorm to a distant asteroid and summoned Galactus to join them. Galactus realized that Hyperstorm's energies could satisfy his hunger and started to feed. Reed banished them to a pocket universe. Galactus eventually returned, but Hyperstorm's fate is currently unknown.

I HAVE NO DESIRE TO ENGAGE YOU IN FRUITLESS *COMBAT*, MORTAL!

AARRGNN!

Heroes Reborn

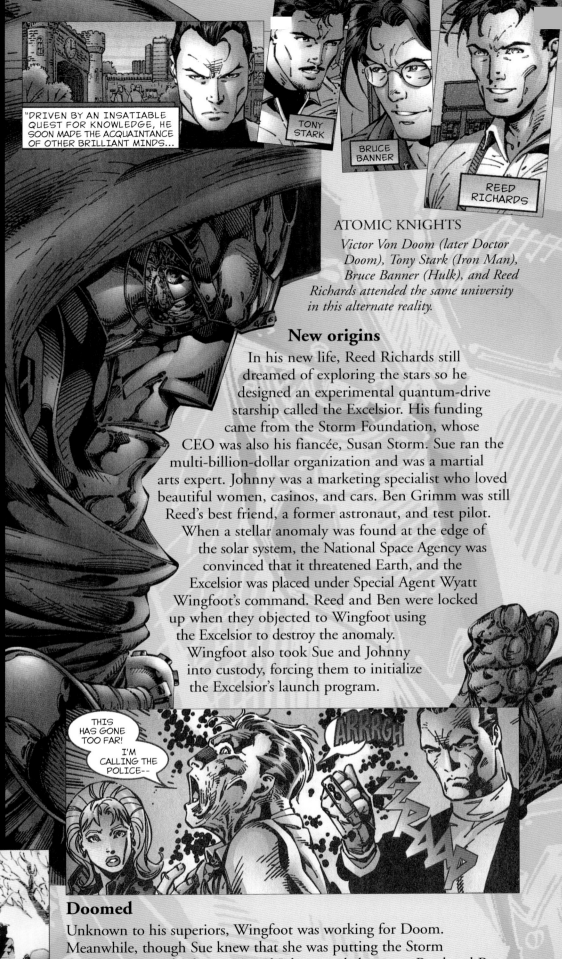

FOR MANY years the X-Men struggled to achieve harmony between men and mutants. Any hope they had seemed doomed when a mutant menace called Onslaught threatened humanity. A being of pure psionic energy and physical prowess, he kidnapped Franklin Richards. The Fantastic Four joined with the X-Men, the Avengers, Spider-Man, the Hulk, and others to prevent Onslaught from turning the human race into a collective consciousness. Franklin was rescued during the final battle when the FF and the Avengers sacrificed themselves to save the world by causing Onslaught to implode. The greatest heroes were no more…or so it seemed.

CHILD POWER

Franklin used his psionic energy to warp reality and shunt his parents, Ben, Johnny, and the Avengers into a pocket universe where they would be safe. With no memory of the past, they could start over and be reborn ….

"DRIVEN BY AN INSATIABLE QUEST FOR KNOWLEDGE, HE SOON MADE THE ACQUAINTANCE OF OTHER BRILLIANT MINDS…"

TONY STARK

BRUCE BANNER

REED RICHARDS

ATOMIC KNIGHTS

Victor Von Doom (later Doctor Doom), Tony Stark (Iron Man), Bruce Banner (Hulk), and Reed Richards attended the same university in this alternate reality.

New origins

In his new life, Reed Richards still dreamed of exploring the stars so he designed an experimental quantum-drive starship called the Excelsior. His funding came from the Storm Foundation, whose CEO was also his fiancée, Susan Storm. Sue ran the multi-billion-dollar organization and was a martial arts expert. Johnny was a marketing specialist who loved beautiful women, casinos, and cars. Ben Grimm was still Reed's best friend, a former astronaut, and test pilot. When a stellar anomaly was found at the edge of the solar system, the National Space Agency was convinced that it threatened Earth, and the Excelsior was placed under Special Agent Wyatt Wingfoot's command. Reed and Ben were locked up when they objected to Wingfoot using the Excelsior to destroy the anomaly. Wingfoot also took Sue and Johnny into custody, forcing them to initialize the Excelsior's launch program.

THIS HAS GONE TOO FAR! I'M CALLING THE POLICE--

ARRRGH

Doomed

Unknown to his superiors, Wingfoot was working for Doom. Meanwhile, though Sue knew that she was putting the Storm Foundation at risk, she convinced Johnny to help rescue Reed and Ben. They were soon reunited, but it was too late. Wingfoot had armed the Excelsior in order to destroy the anomaly. If it were a message from space, Reed feared that the government's aggressive actions might doom the Earth, so the four raced to prepare a prototype for launch.

Super Heroes again

As the Excelsior rocketed into space, Reed and his friends entered a makeshift spacecraft. Knowing that they lacked the fuel reserves and reinforced shielding of the Excelsior, the team was not sure they would survive their trip. But they were willing to sacrifice themselves to save their planet. They reached the anomaly moments before Wingfoot fired his missiles. Exposed to the combined radiation of the missiles, space, and the anomaly, the team crashed on Earth. They soon discovered that they had all gained superhuman powers and pledged to pool their new abilities as the Fantastic Four.

SECRET SKRULL

The FF later discovered that the man they thought was Wyatt Wingfoot was actually a Skrull masquerading as the government agent. Pretending to work for Doctor Doom, the Skrull captured the Silver Surfer. He later became a Super-Skrull when he betrayed Doom and hijacked the Surfer's cosmic power for himself.

MY HAND'S-- TURNING INTO-- ROCK! CAN'T -- FEEL -- ANYTHING!

KRRRKLE

I CAN *ATTUNE* MYSELF TO ALL YOUR DIFFERENT POWERS AND THEN USE THEM IN ANY *COMBINATION* AGAINST YOU!

WAM

THE SILVER ANOMALY

The new FF discovered that the stellar anomaly was the Silver Surfer. Instead of destroying him, Wingfoot had used the missile strike to cover the Surfer's abduction. Wingfoot turned his captive over to Doctor Doom, who interrogated the alien and tried to steal his power. Doom learned that the Galactus of this reality planted catalyst pods in worlds around the universe. The pods gradually mutated planets so that they could sustain Galactus. The Surfer had come to Earth to see if it was ready to be devoured.

YOU'RE *RIGHT*, SUE. I BELIEVE A FANTASTIC TWIST OF FATE BROUGHT THE FOUR OF US TOGETHER...

...AND IMBUED EACH OF US WTH INCREDIBLE POWERS. TO WHAT ULTIMATE *PURPOSE* OR *DESTINY*, I CANNOT SAY...

BUT OUR FIRST CHALLENGE IS *CLEAR*, AND WE'VE NO TIME TO WASTE! NEW YORK CITY IS IN DIRE NEED OF THE UNIQUE *TALENTS* OF THE... *...FANTASTIC FOUR*

COOL NAME, REED!

YOU KNOW GUYS, THIS SUPER-HERO GIG COULD BE A GREAT *MARKETING* GIMMICK!

I MEAN ALL WE NEED NOW ARE SOME HIP-HAPPENIN' CODE NAMES.

SHOULDA FIGURED *YOU'D* COME UP WITH SOME SORTA *LICENSING* ANGLE TO MAKE *MONEY* OFF OF THIS.

Old faces, new agendas

The new FF also met the Mole Man, who was now a religious fanatic determined to conquer the world; the Sub-Mariner, who attacked the surface world because he feared that it was responsible for the pollution that was slowly poisoning his people; and the Black Panther, a head-of-state who often conducted business with Susan. Other old faces included the Inhumans, who were now the remnants of an ancient civilization that predated man, and Maximus, who belonged to the same cult as the Mole Man.

THE HEROES RETURN

Reed led his team into the Negative Zone, where he met Uatu. He showed the FF images from other timelines. Sue was shocked to see that she and Reed had a son in an alternate dimension. Images of Franklin began to haunt her dreams. Back on the real Earth, Franklin believed that his parents were still alive, causing his pocket universe to become unstable. Realizing that they did not belong in this alternate dimension, the Avengers and the FF returned to their plane of reality.

WHAT'S CRUCIBLE-- *DOING*-- TO ME?

MY MIND-- FEELS LIKE IT'S ON *FIRE!*

Crucible

DOUBLE DOOM
Reed mistook Crucible for Doom. Crucible thought it would be apt if he destroyed the doctor's enemy.

THE **E**NCLAVE is a group who want to create an artificial race ruled by dictatorship with the aim of ridding the world of war and crime. Two of its members, nuclear physicist Maris Morlak and geneticist Wladyslav Shinsky, would each come to inhabit the armor of Crucible, created by the Monks of Doom, in a bid to harness Reed's creative energy to further their cause. They believed their ideas would be humanity's salvation.

Crushing Crucible

To trap Reed, Morlak as Crucible attacked a meeting of scientists, forcing Reed to come to the rescue. Activating a device, Crucible was able to tap into Reed's energies. He then took Reed to Genosha, where Crucible experimented on Genoshans. The Genoshan government captured Reed to help them against Crucible, not realizing Reed had lost his powers.

Mind-swap

The rest of the FF searched for Reed. Crucible swapped their minds with three Genoshans so they could not use their powers. However, after a fight with their counterparts, they reclaimed their bodies. Shinsky became Crucible and was defeated later by Reed.

NOT SO FANTASTIC
Jomo Kimane, Farisa Mansour, and Harry Soong were the unlikely vessels for the minds of Ben, Sue, and Johnny.

I BID YOU WELCOME --

-- YOU ONCE AND FORMER MEMBERS OF THE *FANTASTIC FOUR* --

-- TO YOUR NEW *HOME*...

...*JOMO KIMANE*...

...*FARISA MANSOUR*...

...*HARRY SOONG* --

...AND YOUR NEW *LIVES!*

THIS IS THE *CREEP* YOU TOLD US ABOUT BEN -

-- THE ONE YOU AND REED FOUGHT IN *STOCKHOLM!*

SEE FF #5.

Marvel Girl

VALERIA VON DOOM is the daughter of Sue Richards and Victor Von Doom in an alternate timeline. One day, Valeria walked out of a bathroom and came face to face with her brother Franklin, who was only five years old. In her reality, he was her older brother! Almost instantly she had to call on her powers to defend Franklin and his babysitter, and became Marvel Girl.

Mutinous Bounty

A bounty hunter conveniently called Bounty was stalking Franklin's babysitter, a Super Heroine named Caledonia. Valeria transformed into Marvel Girl in order to save them. However, before she had the chance, the Bacchäe, Hades' henchmen, captured Marvel Girl, Franklin, aunt Alyssa, and Caledonia. The Fantastic Four rescued Valeria and realized that they had met her in a time where the present and past co-existed.

YOU'RE MY **BIG BROTHER**, YOU'RE NOT SUPPOSED TO BE A **KID**!

OH GLORY, YOU BETTER NOT BE **TIME-DANCING** AGAIN.

YOU KNOW THAT MAKES MOM TOTALLY **TERMINAL**!

YOU'RE **VALERIA**!

LIKE, YOU FINALLY **NOTICED**?

I'VE **SEEN** YOU--IN MY **SPECIAL** DREAMS! WE'VE HAD **ADVENTURES**!

Fantastic family

Reed and Sue were worried that Valeria's presence meant that the future and past that they had seen would come true: Reed, Ben, and Johnny would die, and Sue would be Valeria's mother and Doctor Doom's widow. Fearing rejection, Valeria disappeared and tried to fight various beings, including a mind-controlled Thing. Luckily, Sue came to her rescue and finally accepted Valeria before taking her home.

FAMILY TIES
Initially, Reed and Sue were fearful of what Valeria represented.

MARVELOUS
Marvel Girl's outfit is like a cross between her mother's FF suit and her father's armor.

"ABOUT FIVE OR SO YEARS AGO, THE TEAM SUFFERED ITS MOST DEVASTATING *LOSS.*

"WHILE THE ACTUAL DETAILS WERE NEVER RELEASED TO THE PUBLIC, WE DID LEARN THAT REED AND SUSAN SUFFERED A DREADFUL MISHAP.

Fantastic Five

IN A POSSIBLE future that may never occur, the Fantastic Four fought Hyperstorm in the Negative Zone and Reed was disfigured. Hyperstorm was defeated, but his doomsday weapon ripped a hole in the fabric of reality. Sue's force field stopped the hole from destroying reality. To keep her in suspended animation but retain her force field, Reed created a space station around her.

From the ashes

The rest of the world was unaware that an unconscious woman was all that prevented total oblivion. After months of seclusion, the team formally changed its name to the Fantastic Five and was made up of Johnny Storm, the Human Torch; his shape-shifting wife, Lyja Storm, whose codename was Ms. Fantastic; Franklin Richards, known as Psi-Lord; Ben Grimm, the Thing; and Big Brain, a robot with Reed's brain.

THE FUTURE F5

Torus thinks a future F5 will consist of Jacob, Alyce, Franklin, himself, and Kristoff Vernard (Doom).

Till death

Unable to leave his beloved wife, Reed Richards took up permanent residence in the Fantastistation, the space station he had constructed. He attended to the unconscious Sue while slowly repairing the hole, managing to restore a few inches every month. Knowing that Sue was depending on him, he never stopped trying to find a way to knit the hole together. Reed's only contact with the outside world was through his Big Brain robot.

BIG BRAIN

Using a subspace carrier beam, Reed controls Big Brain from the Negative Zone. His first Big Brain was like HERBIE but he has updated his design.

--BUT I'LL EVENTUALLY FIND A WAY TO KNIT THE ENTIRE HOLE *BACK* TOGETHER.

LISTEN DAD...THIS PLACE IS FULLY AUTOMATED, AND YOU COULD USE A BREAK.

HOW ABOUT RETURNING TO *EARTH* WITH US?

NOT QUITE *EVERYONE!* YOU OWE US AN EXPLANATION, YOUNG MAN!

WHO SAID YOU COULD PLAY *HERO?*

EXACTLY HOW LONG HAVE YOU BEEN PLANNING TO BECOME THIS THIS *SUPER-STORM* CHARACTER?

Continuation

After settling down together, John and Lyja Storm had a son, Torus, who inherited his father's control over fire and his mother's shape-shifting abilities. He occasionally took on the appearance of an adult superhuman that he called Super-Storm. Injured in battle, Ben was fitted with bionic implants. He was divorced from Sharon Ventura and had two teenagers, Jacob and Alyce, who dreamed of joining the team.

Fantastic Four 2099

SPIDER-MAN 2099
Trapped in the future, the team enlists the aid of that era's Spider-Man, but even he cannot discern if they are clones or the real FF.

IN ANOTHER POSSIBLE timeline, the Fantastic Four awoke within a cryogenic suspension chamber in the Negative Zone. After returning to Earth, they discovered that the year was 2099 and the planet was ruled by multi-national corporations instead of governments. One of the largest, Stark/Fujikawa, declared that the FF were genetic experiments that had gone astray and claimed them as escaped property.

Brave new world

On the run from Stark/Fujikawa, the FF met Chimera, a fellow fugitive from the Negative Zone, who volunteered to serve as their guide. Chimera fell in love with Reed and repeatedly attempted to delete Susan from his program. The team stumbled upon a cult that worshiped the mighty Thor and learned that Doctor Doom was trying to free Latveria from corporate control.

Strange tidings

Hoping to learn how and why they came to this timeline, the Fantastic Four attempted to return to the Negative Zone. Their entrance was blocked by Dr. Strange, the master of the mystic arts, who had journeyed into the future to warn them that a planetoid was on a collision course with the Earth. The polar icecaps began to melt, and flood waters spread across the globe. Desperate to save the planet, Reed Richards joined forces with Doom 2099. The Watcher revealed that these FF members were actually temporal copies of the originals, constructed purely to spare the Earth from destruction.

DOOM 2099

Doom 2099 cannot recall how he came to the future, but he claims to be the original Victor Von Doom.

> OKAY, YOU FANTASTIC *FUGITIVES!* TIME FOR A *CRASH COURSE* IN 2099 BY--

> *YEAH,* COBWEB HEAD-- JUST LIKE *YER* GONNA BE IN ABOUT TWO--

> OH, THE GUARDS ARE *GONE?*

The Fantastic Four in the 2000s

Having introduced the future daughter of Sue Richards and Doom from an alternate timeline, Chris Claremont and Salvador Larroca began the decade by exploring how Valeria Von Doom fitted in with the rest of the Fantastic Four family. They also brought back the real Doctor Doom, leaving Reed trapped in Doom's armor and trying to find a way to avert a world war. Writer and artist Carlos Pacheco, with Rafael Marin and later Jeph Loeb, began with Diablo, the destruction of Pier 4, and the return of the Super-Skrull. Pacheco introduced Noah Baxter, Senso, Abraxas, and a new Baxter Building. Ben regained the ability to transform into the Thing at will and Johnny became a movie actor. With the help of most of the comic-book industry, writer and artist Erik Larsen supervised the production of a 12-issue limited series called *The World's Greatest Comic Magazine*, celebrating Stan Lee and Jack Kirby's work. Writer Mark Waid and artist Mike Wieringo introduced Modulus and took a fresh look at familiar FF villains, like the Frightful Four, in the main FF title. New FF-related titles included *Marvel Knights 4*, by Roberto Aguirre-Sacasa and Steve McNiven, which focused on the family aspect of the team. *Ultimate Fantastic Four* by Brian Bendis, Mark Millar, Warren Ellis, Adam Kubert, and Stuart Immonen recreated the team to fit into the Ultimate Universe. The biggest news was the announcement of the major motion picture, produced by Marvel Entertainment and 20th Century Fox and directed by Tim Story.

Fantastic Four Annual *2000*. The Sub-Mariner's ex-girlfriend returns. (Cover by Salvador Larroca and Art Thibert)

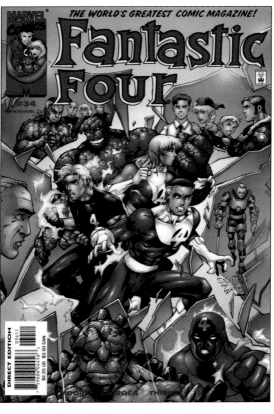

Fantastic Four *Vol. 3 #34 (Oct. 2000). While the rest of the team hunts for an alien saboteur, Sue is trapped in the Wild West. (Cover by Salvador Larroca and Art Thibert)*

2000

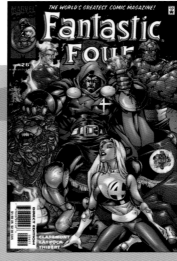

Fantastic Four *Vol. 3 #26 (Feb. 2000). Sue, Johnny, and the Thing try to stop Doom's army (Cover by Salvador Larroca and Art Thibert)*

2001

Fantastic Four *Vol. 3 #47 (Nov. 2001). Alternate realities collide with ours as the FF battle Abraxas. (Cover by Carlos Pacheco and Jesús Merino)*

2002

Fantastic Four *Vol. 3 #60 (Oct. 2002). Mark Waid and Mike Wieringo begin their highly acclaimed run. (Cover by Mike Wieringo and Karl Kesel)*

2003

Fantastic Four *#500 (Sept. 2003). The title celebrates 500 issues by officially returning to the numbering from its first volume. (Cover by Paolo Rivera)*

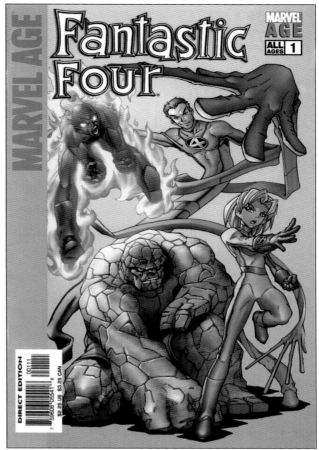

Marvel Age Fantastic Four #1 (July 2004).
*Marvel targets young readers with a new FF title that
retells old Stan Lee and Jack Kirby stories with a
modern twist. (Cover by Makoto Nakatsuka)*

Fantastic Four #27 (March 2000).
*The Super Hero community is shocked when Sue
agrees to be Doom's consort, but she knows
that Reed is the man in the armor.
(Cover by Salvador Larroca and
Maria Pilar)*

June 2004 Oct. 2004 Dec. 2004

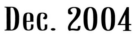

Fantastic Four #512 (June 2004).
*The Human Torch teams up with
everyone's favorite web-swinger. (Cover
by Mike Wieringo and Karl Kesel)*

Fantastic Four #517 (Oct. 2004).
*Aliens invade Earth to destroy the
Invisible Woman. (Cover by Mike
Wieringo and Karl Kesel)*

Fantastic Four #521 (Dec. 2004).
*Galactus's new herald, Johnny
tries to stop Galactus from eating
Earth. (Cover by Mike Wieringo)*

Abraxas

The quest for perfection

THE HEAD OF Galactus unexpectedly fell from space and landed in the middle of New York's Times Square. Reed discovered that the head did not belong to the Galactus he knew. Someone killed a Galactus from another reality and sent it to the Fantastic Four as a warning. Realizing they needed help, the FF went to the Blue Area of the Moon to consult the Watcher. Instead of Uatu, they discovered a Watcher suffering from amnesia. Nova and an intelligent Hulk from an alternate reality arrived and other realities began to bleed in. The FF confronted alternate versions of themselves and learned that a near-omnipotent menace was headed toward Earth, an entity who called himself Abraxas.

REALITY WALKER
Abraxas can assume an ethereal state, which allows him to step from one alternate reality into another. He travels with the speed of thought.

Cleaning universes

Abraxas dreams of a single perfect universe and is dedicated to cleansing the multiverse. He seeks out and eliminates powerful entities that exist on more than one alternate world. He erases planes of reality that do not fit his ideas of perfection. After scouring universes and destroying different versions of Galactus, Reed realized that Abraxas seeks Galactus's weapon, the Ultimate Nullifier, so that he can erase every plane of reality except one.

Scavenger hunt

The FF joined their alternate world doppelgängers in a hunt for the Nullifier that extended across the multiverse. The Human Torch and Nova found the weapon. However, Nova betrayed Johnny and revealed that she worked for Abraxas. As Nova delivered the Nullifier to her new master, Franklin Richards and Marvel Girl combined powers to summon the real Galactus. Reed got the Nullifier, turning it on Abraxas and restoring the universe to its proper state.

POWER PERSONIFIED
Abraxas possesses a level of cosmic power that is totally beyond human comprehension. He can restructure molecules and convert physical matter into pure energy. He can project concussive blasts powerful enough to shatter an entire galaxy and has destroyed entire planes of reality.

HIDE IN PLAIN SIGHT

Since most of the Hidden look like normal humans, they have found it relatively easy to infiltrate governments and places of power. Whenever there is the slightest chance that their race will be discovered, they use their powers to influence world leaders to create scandals or wars, focusing attention in other directions.

Senso Sweet revenge

A FEW THOUSAND years ago, a group of Inhumans began to develop the ability to influence the minds and emotions of those around them. Distrusted and feared, this group eventually left the Great Refuge. They mated with humans, blending in with each generation. A group of Nazi explorers found this group in 1942. The Nazis killed the adults and captured the children. Tortured and enslaved, those who survived the Nazi death camps realized that they must make sure that they could never be found. They called themselves the Hidden, and their leader was named Senso.

A choice of dooms

The Fantastic Four were alerted when ruler Black Bolt and his royal family returned from a mission in space. The Inhumans had come before the UN to establish peaceful relations with humanity. Fearing that their distant relatives might reveal their existence, the Hidden, with their ghostly glowing eyes, secretly used their powers of persuasion to turn the world against the Inhumans. In his human form, Ben Grimm attempted to find who was behind the anti-Inhuman fervor and was captured by Senso. When the UN rejected Black Bolt, Doctor Doom offered the Inhumans asylum in Latveria.

The eyes have it

While searching for Ben, Reed was also taken prisoner. He discovered that Senso wears many guises and can appear as either a hardworking military aide or a sultry rebel leader. Since she intended to bury Reed and Ben in a military prison for the rest of their lives, Senso taunted them, revealing that the Hidden blame the Inhumans for all their suffering. By sheer force of will, Ben managed to free himself and Reed from Senso's control, forcing her to flee. Senso's current whereabouts are unknown, and the Hidden still live among us.

GREY GARGOYLE

Paul Duval was a chemist who spilled a chemical on his left hand. It turned into living stone and gained the power to transform anything it touched into stone. Tired of a life of crime, Duval agreed to work for Senso.

Senso can manipulate thoughts and emotions, fire mental blasts that cause intense physical agony, and alter the way people see her so that different individuals see a different woman.

I KNOW IT'S BEEN A WHILE SINCE OUR *LAST* ENCOUNTER, SIR BUT I AM QUITE CERTAIN MINE IS A NAME YOU WILL REMEMBER FOR A *LONG* TIME TO COME...

...ONCE YOU *REAWAKEN!*

Modulus

SUPER-PDA
Reed Richards' PDA has an infinite storage capacity. It uses a subspace transmission to download data directly into a neighboring dimension of pure electromagnetic energy.

JEALOUS BECAUSE his parents were spending time with his sister, Franklin Richards tried to win back their attention by becoming smarter. He took his father's Super-PDA, on which Reed jotted down all his thoughts. This device was a conduit to another dimension, and Franklin unleashed a living mathematical equation from it. Calling itself Modulus, the being claimed that it was in love with Reed and wanted to bond itself to him.

Murderous math

Considering itself to be the mathematical equivalent of Reed and the total of his essence, Modulus realized that it was the only one worthy of him. It decided to subtract anyone competing for Reed's affections and attacked Sue and Ben. It divided molecules and tried to reduce them into their chemical components. Saved by Sue's force fields, Sue and Ben escaped. Reed confronted Modulus, who linked their minds until the Torch drove them apart.

ADAPTABLE
An electrochemical creature, Modulus can assume any shape it desires. It uses radio waves to transmit itself to any FF communications device.

Balancing act
Reed realized that Modulus was lonely because it was only half of an equation. It could never rest until it found an equal who could balance it. Ordering the others to distract the creature, Reed entered the alien dimension that birthed Modulus and began to fashion another mathematical duplicate of himself.

The correct answer

Ben and Johnny tried to lead Modulus into an abandoned building, but it multiplied the structure's molecules, until the building collapsed. When Modulus returned to the Baxter Building, Reed offered it the new double, but it rejected the copy—it wanted the original. Citing his love for Franklin, Reed stated that he and Modulus could never balance each other. So, Modulus formed a stable equation with the double and went home.

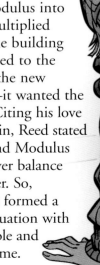

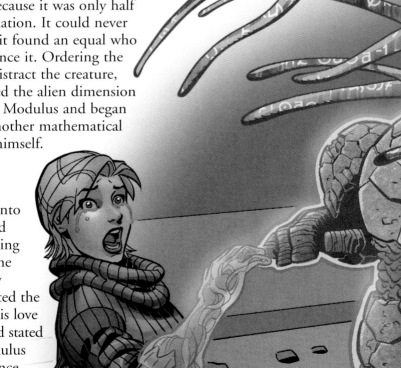

Johnny the Invisible Boy

FOUR ALIEN obelisks descended from the sky and surrounded Manhattan. The Fantastic Four discovered that a federation of aliens whose worlds had been consumed by Galactus had developed a technology that could cloak planets. They had come to Earth because they learned that someone could negate their device. The aliens wanted to destroy this person before Galactus could find her. Her name was Sue Richards, and she could make invisible things visible.

Trading places

When the aliens threatened to destroy the city unless Sue surrendered, Reed invented a weapon that seemed to take away her powers. Since Sue was no longer a danger, the aliens left and Reed revealed that his weapon switched powers between Sue and Johnny. Sue was the Human Torch, and Johnny was the Invisible Boy.

Rising Storm

While the team were celebrating their deception, Galactus arrived, snatched Johnny, and gave him the "power cosmic." Realizing that Galactus intended to use Johnny as his new herald, the FF enlisted the aid of Quasar and gave chase. Knowing that Galactus would soon need to feed, Johnny tested his powers as he scoured the universe for an uninhabited world.

Galen's return

The FF found Johnny and used a variation of Reed's power-switching machine to strip Galactus of all his cosmic energy. Galactus became Galen again. Knowing this change would not last, the FF brought Galen back to Earth and tried to convince him to stop devouring inhabited worlds. Galen exiled himself in an energy-rich dimension so that the rest of the universe would be safe from Galactus—forever.

Unthinkable

VICTOR Von Doom had been perfectly content protecting the people of Latveria from harm and fighting against the Fantastic Four using any means that science and technology would allow. He had discovered early on that his mother had been a sorceress but picked science over magic as his weapon of choice. However, his priorities changed. Doom began his pursuit of sorcery, sacrificing anything and anyone necessary in order to become the greatest magician. How would Reed Richards, the man who believes everything has a scientific explanation, cope with Doctor Doom's rejection of science in favor of magic? Would he be able to defend his team against something that he felt was impossible, unbelievable, and unthinkable?

Love's young dream

Two young Hungarian gypsies, Valerie and Victor, fell in love and meant the world to each other. But Victor became interested in new technologies as a way of protecting his village and was awarded with a U.S. scholarship. This was the beginning of a new life for Victor—but without Valeria. She felt she should could not leave her home. Victor went to America and threw himself into work. While there, he suffered a disfigurement and vowed to spend his life avenging it. After years of using his technologies for evil, Victor decided he wanted to find Valeria and renounce science. Using fortune-tellers, Victor tracked Valeria down and tried to win her back. But his intentions were not as pure as they seemed.

LOVE TOKEN

In order to prove the honesty of his feelings for Valeria, Victor gives her a locket that he has treasured since they parted. He convinces Valeria that she must still love him as she does not flinch from him when he removes his mask. Valeria takes Victor's hand—with explosive consequences.

AAH! VICTOR!

> Valeria knows full well the man I have since become. So disapproving is she that she lives in hiding...striving to ensure our paths never again...

NEW ARMOR

Valeria's body bursts into flames, and her skin unravels and envelops Victor. As Valeria meets her doom, Victor explains that he had made the wrong choice— however, it wasn't choosing science over Valeria but choosing science over sorcery.

Evil pact

Doom made a bargain with demons in hell to make him the best magician he could be—and Valeria was the sacrifice. Meanwhile, baby Valeria Richards was playing with her building blocks when Doom appeared in one of them. He explained that Valeria, the child he named, is his "familiar"—his eyes and ears for his magic. Doom vowed that Reed would die. But first Doom and the demons kidnapped Franklin Richards and took him to hell.

VICTOR'S VESSEL

Doom explains to Valeria Richards the link that will always bind them: despite Reed's help, Sue suffered a miscarriage during her first pregnancy. When she became pregnant again, she went into labor when Reed was away. Johnny Storm called on Doom for help. Doom agreed, but only if he could name the child after his lost love. Doom cast a series of spells to bind this Valeria to him—forever.

DEMONIC

The Haazareth Three supply Doom with sorcerous powers in return for Doom becoming their representative on Earth. Doom uses the demons to help abduct Franklin, ensuring the Fantastic Four follow in hot pursuit.

Science versus sorcery

The Fantastic Four boarded a ship to rescue Franklin, but the ship crashed right into Doom's path. Doom's power had grown even stronger. Doom locked Reed in a prison to teach him about magic—he could only escape by casting the correct spell. Although he was opposed to this, Reed realized that it was not enough merely to say the spell; he had to believe in it and accept that there were some things beyond scientific analysis. He worked out that he could enchant only by admitting his foolishness when it came to sorcery. The FF rescued Franklin and all of the team except Reed returned through the portal.

CHANGE OF HEART?

Doom denies he is indebted to anyone, and the Haazareth Three pull him back toward hell. Apologizing to Reed, Doom begs for help, but Reed does not fall for Doom's lies. As Reed is about to turn to go, Doom reaches out to him and dramatically scars his face. However, the mental scars are far greater, and Reed retreats into himself.

Damaged

To attempt to get Reed to channel his anger, Johnny time-traveled with him back to Hungary and tried to get him to kill Victor. He could not do it but did shoot at him, taking a lock of Victor's hair to experiment on. Meanwhile, Franklin felt he was still in hell. The family realized that he preferred this imaginary world to the real world where people might not always rescue you. The FF had been changed—forever.

Authoritative Action

IN A BATTLE for the souls of Franklin and Valeria, Reed Richards finally defeated his arch-enemy, Doctor Doom, and exiled him to a demonic dimension—but the victory was not without cost. Doom tortured the Fantastic Four, destroyed their home, and disfigured Reed Richards. While the team were still reeling from these injuries, a new problem arose. Doom was the absolute monarch of Latveria, providing his people with food, housing, and free health care. Doom demanded blind obedience in return. Who would lead and protect his homeland now that he was gone? Who would gain control of Doom's scientific wonders and advanced weapons of mass destruction? While debates raged in the United Nations over the "Latverian problem," the countries along its borders prepared to invade….

WITH POWER…
From the sidelines, Reed grows more concerned. He knows that the world is better off without Doom but fears for Latveria. He does not trust politicians to stand up for the country and knows its small army cannot protect it from invasion. He fears that Super Villains may try to loot Doom's weaponry. He wonders who will take responsibility for the Latverian people.

Taking responsiblity
Believing that Latveria rested on land stolen from it, Hungary launched its first attack against the seemingly defenseless country. The invaders were repelled when the FF joined the Latverians. Tanks were crushed, munitions were set aflame, and entire divisions were trapped within invisible force fields. Warning the Hungarians that he would hit their government with a debilitating computer virus if they returned, Reed sent them into retreat.

Instead of thanking the Fantastic Four, the Latverians turn against them. Doom had always taken care of his people, giving them everything they needed. He was their leader and protector. Thanks to the way Doom had always portrayed the FF, the Latverians fear them and see little difference between them and any other foreign invaders.

> One week ago, with the help of my family--my wife, Susan Richards, my brother-in-law, Johnny Storm, and my friend Ben Grimm--I defeated your former ruler of many years, Victor Von Doom, in final combat.

> For that, I am genuinely convinced no apology is required. Though my family and I believe unequivocally in the sanctity of human life--

These fears are only heightened when Reed Richards later declares himself sovereign of Latveria in order to fill the power vacuum left by Doom. The rest of the world is shocked, but the Latverians expected no less.

Fearing that Doom will return, Reed decides to leave the former ruler with nothing. He aims to dismantle Doom's technology, destroy his weapons, and give away his fortune. Reed will strip away Doom's resources so that he will never again be able to threaten the FF.

> I'm sure the U.N. will sort out what to do here sooner than later, but I'm not going to watch blood be spilled while they debate.

> Nor am I eager to let any attacking army seize Victor's unguarded technology--

Political unrest

Even though Reed granted total freedom to all Latverians, a resistance movement began to grow within the country. Johnny and Ben tracked down the rebels but were later enraged when robots sent by Reed attacked and jailed them. Relations with Reed grew even more strained when he sent his robots into the streets. The team also learned that the United States had disavowed Reed's actions in Latveria and intended to arrest him for treason.

It's a little Mobius dimension I invented a few years ago:

Infinite—

—and, at the same time, very, very finite.

There's no way out.

For either of us.

With me, Victor.

And I promise you:

you only thought you were in Hell.

Reed...?

Perpetual prison

After alienating the rest of the team and sending them away, Reed entered a special chamber and transported himself to a pocket dimension—from which there could be no escape—and summoned the spirit of Doctor Doom to join him. In order to ensure that his family and friends would remain free from Doom, Reed had decided to sacrifice himself and serve as Doom's jailer for all eternity.

MIND-JUMPING

The rest of the FF is not willing to lose Reed. As they try to rescue him from the prison dimension, they unintentionally free Doom. Doom uses his ability to move his mind into another's body and seizes control of Sue. With her powers at his command, he races outside and is shocked at the changes Reed has made to his Latveria.

I always said Susan was more powerful than the three of you put together...

Bitter victory

After mind-jumping from the Invisible Woman to the Human Torch, Doom grew even more desperate when he learned that Reed had disposed of his backup weapons, his spare armor, and his personal fortune. Seeing that he had truly lost everything, Doom realized that there was still one way for him to win his final battle with Reed Richards. Doom mind-jumped into Ben's body and threatened to use the Thing's strength to kill Johnny and Sue. Reed had no choice. The only way he could finally stop Doom was by killing his best friend. With tears in his eyes, Reed Richards pulled the trigger.

BENNNNNNN!

Hereafter

IN AN ATTEMPT to defeat Doctor Doom once and for all, Reed Richards banished the Latverian ruler to Hell, but was severely scarred in the process. In order to prevent Doom's advanced technology falling into the wrong hands, he then organized a coup d'état in Latveria. United Nation forces led by Colonel Nick Fury were sent in to undo Reed's actions, but it soon became clear that his claim to Latveria was all part of his plan to imprison Doom forever. But when Ben Grimm's body was possessed by Doom's spirit, Richards was forced to fight his teammate. Reed managed to destroy Doom's consciousnness, but at a terrible price—the death of his best friend.

Medical research

After the Thing was mortally wounded in the battle at Castle Doom, Mr. Fantastic attempted resuscitation and heart massage for over an hour. Forced to accept their friend's death, the FF said farewell to Ben in a closed-casket funeral. However, Ben had signed a contract with the U.S. military that allowed them to study his mutated body in the event of his death. Stealing the Thing's body from the Walter Reed Army Medical Center, Richards placed it in a special preservation tank.

--and it blew up in Victor Von Doom's face.

Von Doom's machine

Finding a spark of life still dwelling within Ben's brain, Reed began to formulate a plan. He believed that Ben's consciousness had transmigrated to another plane of existence—in other words, the Thing had gone to Heaven. Working on the principle that energy cannot be destroyed, only transformed or relocated, saving Ben would be a simple matter of retrieving the energy that formed his consciousness. To do this, Richards planned to use the machine Von Doom had created in his college days to contact his dead mother.

UNSTABLE DEVICE

Reed Richards had warned Doom about his machine's instability, but he refused to listen. The machine blew up in the Latverian's face, creating a permanent scar.

You're positive that this machine is stable? What if it blows up in your face, too?

RESCUING BEN

Wary of the dangers of Doom's machine, Sue Richards was unsure whether the mission to rescue Ben was a good idea. Eventually deciding to take the risk, she and Johnny joined hands with Reed as he pulled the lever to activate the device.

HUH

Then I've got nothing to lose.

FLAMING ASSAULT

In Heaven, the FF teammates were attacked by a flying horde of winged, hooded angels brandishing flaming swords. Despite a valiant battle, Mr. Fantastic, the Invisible Woman, and the Human Torch were nearly overcome by the assailants. As the FF appeared on the verge of defeat, their attackers disappeared. Richards surmised that the purpose of the assault had been to give them a "divine warning."

WRITTEN WARNING

Reed confronted the angels to make it clear that the FF came in peace. The attackers let the FF know that they were not welcome in Heaven. The angels had been sent by Ben, who was reunited with his brother, Daniel. Daniel had died, but the brothers had met again in Heaven.

The door to the afterlife

Theorizing that their environment was being shaped by the desires of whoever was in the lead, the teammates encounted several different situations. When Reed led, the team had to cross a gigantic puzzle. Sue's lead took them home, while Johnny's reality recreated a childhood camping trip. Finally, the FF found Ben, who had been reunited with his dead brother, Daniel. Ben was not yet in Heaven proper, which lay beyond a metal door. Ben believed Richards was keeping his body alive artificially on Earth, and that Reed had created the door to stop Ben entering the afterlife beyond. However, Ben later realized that, as he himself had arrived at the door first, it must have been his own mind that created the barrier.

Meeting the maker

When Ben realized his true desire was to return to Earth, he said goodbye to Daniel. Invited into Heaven proper to meet God, the FF were amazed to find out that he "sketched out" reality in the same way as a comic-book artist. Redrawing Ben so that he once again resembled the Thing, God then "re-drew" the FF's world, transporting them home.

Ultimate Fantastic Four

IN AN ALTERNATE reality, studious Reed Richards was the victim of bullying, at home, at the hands of his father, and at school. Ben Grimm came to his rescue when a group of boys were forcing Reed's head down a toilet, and, in return, Reed showed Ben his latest scientific finding. Reed had discovered that there was another plane of existence that was very close to our own. He planned to send toys and candy bars to this other dimension to find out if there was life there—just as soon as he could work out how to break the barrier between the two planes.

GRIMM REAPER
Reed explained his discovery of alternate dimensions to Ben, but Ben had great trouble getting his head around it. He just wanted help with his trigonometry homework!

Talent scout

Six months later at the school science fair, Reed was ready to exhibit his experiment. He believed it could change the world, enabling starving people to have food transported to them instantly. For now, though, Reed only transported a toy car. The dramatic disappearance of the car amazed everyone, especially a Mainland Technology Development scout who recommended that Reed attend a "think tank" of other talented young people.

Baxter Building

Reed was sent to the Baxter Building where he met Dr. Storm and his children, Johnny and Sue. He was told that Dr. Storm had found the co-ordinates to the alternate plane or N-Zone but that Reed was the first person to actually break through the barrier.

Miscalculation

Whilst at the Baxter Building, Reed also met Victor Von Doom. Victor was a loner who idolized Dr. Molekevic, one of the teachers. One day, Reed returned to his room and found Victor working on Reed's calculations. Initially angry, Reed realized that Victor was right about some of the computations. They agreed to call a truce so they could work on the project together, provided Victor promised to be nice!

MOLE MAN
Dr. Molekevic (Mole Man) was fired after it was found that he was working on illegal bio-technology to create bizarre life forms.

When Reed tested his theories, the result was an explosion that scattered the FF across the world and gave them powers.

Water: Mr. Fantastic

Reed was almost shot at by officers when they first saw him, not realizing who he was. The scientist's limbs had elongated as if they were made of water. As the fate of the others came to light, Reed realized that their new forms represented the different elements. He also discovered that this freak accident was caused by someone tampering with the computer and his calculations.

Rock: The Thing

Ben was discovered in Mexico City, where his increase in physical strength caused trucks to crash when they drove into him. Reed told Ben that his new form was due to a suit that he had to wear to protect the world from the extra impact he was putting on the planet. Ben blamed Reed for this metamorphosis into the Thing.

Fire: The Human Torch

Johnny woke up to find himself in a European hospital with the ability to engulf himself in flames with no risk of injury. The Human Torch honed his skill of commanding fire by simply uttering, "Flame on!"

GRIMM'S TALES
Ben was found by two children. He had great difficulty accepting his new condition.

Doomed

Reed, Ben, and Johnny were engaged in a battle with a monster that led them to Moleman's lair and to Sue. Moleman set his clay creatures on them and, despite Reed's pleas, turned against his students. Reed decided they must excavate Mole Man's den with Victor's help. But Victor was now horribly scarred and only wanted revenge on the newly formed FF.

Air: Invisible Woman

The only person who knew where Sue had gone was Mole Man, who had taken her to his lair beneath the Baxter Building. Sue now had the power of invisibility, which she had trouble controlling. Mole Man showed her his video wall that he used to spy on the group. He told the Invisible Woman of his plans to work with her and Victor to uncover life's mysteries.

Marvel Knights 4

> Your total net worth.

> But that's --

> --chump change!

AFTER ALIENATING most of the world for staging a coup d'état in Latveria and being portrayed as traitors in the American press, the Fantastic Four faced a new problem. Reed Richards was forced to sign over the proceeds of all his patents to the government to pay for the expenses incurred by his authoritative actions, and Congress refused to fund any more of his scientific research. To make matters even worse, the value of all of the stocks and bonds in the FF's portfolio had declined because of a weak stock market, and their money manager had swindled them out of all their cash reserves. The Fantastic Four were broke.

From the lows to the Heights

A letter from the mayor told the team that New York City wanted payment for all the damage that the Fantastic Four had "caused" over the years. The mayor offered to forgive the debt if the FF vacated the Baxter Building and turned it over to the city. Forced to lay off all their employees and liquidate their financial assets, the FF held a massive sale to sell most of their possessions. All of the money was given to the families of their former employees. Needing a new place to stay, the Fantastic Four moved into a rundown hotel in Washington Heights.

New careers

After refusing to accept loans from the Avengers and Tony Stark, Reed informed the rest of the team that they had to find work. Sue Richards took a job teaching English at a local high school on the Upper West Side. The students proved unruly at first, but she soon won them over. Though he appeared to have trouble adjusting to his new life, Reed took a temporary job as a computer technician. On the way to work one morning, he talked a lonely stranger out of committing suicide. This made Reed realize that at least he still had his family and things were not so bad as they may have seemed.

EVICTED!
The FF's bad finances drove them from the Baxter Building—something their enemies could not do.

Demolition man

An expert at smashing things, the Thing applied for work in construction. He was refused at first but was hired when he saved workers from being crushed by falling debris. Ben Grimm's strength was an asset on the construction site, but his fellow workers warned him to take it easy. They feared he would put them out of work by completing the job too soon.

Fighting fire with fire

Johnny Storm approached the local firehouse and asked if he could become an apprentice firefighter. The fire chief warned him that the work was not glamorous. A lot of the time it was just grunt work, but Johnny was determined to get the job. The other firefighters were not happy with their new recruit, blaming him for all the times that they had to clean up messes left behind by the Fantastic Four and the city's other Super Heroes. However, Johnny eventually won their respect when he helped a distraught mother retrieve the body of her son.

The Pine Barrens

Reed, Sue, and Ben took Franklin Richards and a group of his friends on a camping trip to the New Jersey Pine Barrens, an untouched, 1,000-square-mile wilderness area. The locals warned Sue to stay away because of a legendary monster, the mysterious Jersey Devil, that was supposed to haunt the region. The Fantastic Four also encountered a pair of filmmakers who were producing a documentary on the creature.

Predators among the pines

When people started to disappear, Sue took charge of defending the children while Reed and Ben searched the area. They stumbled upon a spacecraft that was swarming with an army of vicious-looking aliens. Using his stretching powers to look like one of the creatures, Reed sneaked aboard the ship to rescue the captives. After driving the aliens away, Sue learned that they had been coming to the area for centuries. They had an understanding with the locals and only kidnapped campers and tourists.

Ordinary heroes

Following a fight with Psycho-Man, Reed revealed that he had been using the FF's bankruptcy as a chance for them to be ordinary. Though Reed was pleased at the way everyone had blossomed, Sue convinced him that it was time to reassume their normal lives.

The world of the Fantastic Four

Stockholm •

SWEDEN

Copenhagen •
DENMARK

NETHERLANDS

GERMANY

Paris •
FRANCE

While in Stockholm to attend a scientific symposium, Reed Richards and Ben Grimm first encountered the man known only as Crucible.

RUSSIA

TRANSYLVANIA

HUNGARY

Saragossa •
SPAIN

Saragossa was the birthplace of Esteban Diablo.

Europe
France—The Fantastic Four prevented an alien invasion when an ancient portal to another dimension was discovered under the streets of Paris.

Suffering from amnesia, Medusa was found by the Wizard on the southern coast of France. He invited her to join the Frightful Four.

Denmark—From his base in Copenhagen, Dr. Doom gathered a misfit army and made plans to destroy the FF.

Germany—Having gained the Silver Surfer's cosmic powers, Dr. Doom battled the FF at the foot of the Alps.

Balkans—The tiny kingdom of Latveria on Hungary's southern border was ruled with an iron fist by Dr. Doom.

Transua, Dragorin is the birthplace of the Puppet Master.

Hungary—The Hungarian government invaded Latveria when the FF appeared to have destroyed Dr. Doom.

Netherlands—Ulysses Klaw was born in Vlaardingen.

Transylvania—The FF accidentally stumbled upon the castle of Diablo, where the alchemist was held prisoner.

Russia—Ivan Kragoff left Russia and exposed himself to cosmic radiation in space to become the Red Ghost.

EGYPT

INDIA

TIBET

JAPAN

AFRICA

AUSTRALIA

Egypt
Believing that the ancient Egyptians had a cure for blindness, the FF used Dr. Doom's time machine and journeyed to the ancient land of the pharaohs, where they first encountered Rama-Tut.

Returning to the land of his birth, the Sphinx challenged Galactus to a battle to the death.

Africa
Ruled by the Black Panther, the kingdom of Wakanda is hidden in the jungles of northern Africa.

The Human Torch and the Thing invaded the small kingdom of Rudyarda when they learned that the Black Panther had been imprisoned as an enemy of the state.

India
The Sphinx heard of a wizard whose powers rival his own and searched for him in a secret temple hidden deep within the Himalayan Mountains. There he encountered a mystical entity who foretold his destruction at the hands of Galactus.

After their home in the Andes was discovered by the FF, the Inhumans moved Attilan into the Himalayas.

Tibet
Victor von Doom learned the secrets of sorcery from a mysterious order of monks. They built him an armored suit and mask to hide his scarred face.

Japan
When a giant robot rampaged through Japan, the FF raced to Mount Fujimoto to confront the Samurai Destroyer.

"What gives this family its purpose and its joy isn't the destination... it's the journey."

Arctic

When their powers suddenly began to malfunction, the FF journeyed to the Arctic Circle, where they found an ancient civilization ruled by a blind god.

The FF headed for the northern magnetic pole when they learned that aliens planned to reverse the polarity of the Earth's magnetic field.

United States

California—Launching their experimental starship from Central City, Reed, Sue, Johnny, and Ben were exposed to cosmic radiation and became the FF.

After going bankrupt, the FF went to Los Angeles where they made a movie that was funded by Prince Namor, the Sub-Mariner.

New York City—The home and headquarters of the FF.

After suddenly appearing in Central Park, a mysterious structure teleported the FF to a distant galaxy where the Beyonder forced them to fight in a secret war.

New England—Reed and Sue hired Agatha Harkness to be Franklin's nanny and moved him into her home at Whisper Hill.

Florida—The FF temporarily lost their powers after being exposed to the radiation of a bomb triggered by the Frightful Four on a small atoll off the coast of Florida.

New Mexico—When someone began to sabotage his missile base, General Thaddeus E. Ross asked the FF to investigate, and they soon found themselves in a battle with the incredible Hulk.

South Pacific

While on vacation to a seemingly deserted South Pacific Island, the FF were attacked by the Sentry Sinister, who was left on this planet countless millennia ago by the Kree.

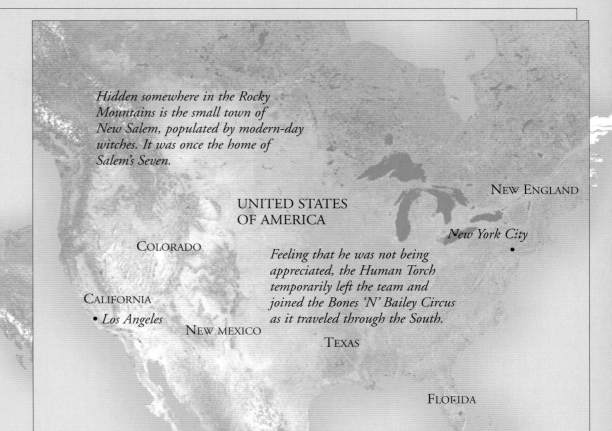

Hidden somewhere in the Rocky Mountains is the small town of New Salem, populated by modern-day witches. It was once the home of Salem's Seven.

NEW ENGLAND

UNITED STATES OF AMERICA

New York City

COLORADO

Feeling that he was not being appreciated, the Human Torch temporarily left the team and joined the Bones 'N' Bailey Circus as it traveled through the South.

CALIFORNIA

Los Angeles

NEW MEXICO

TEXAS

FLORIDA

Bermuda Triangle

At the very center of the Bermuda Triangle lies Monster Isle, the home of the Mole Man and his army of giant creatures.

Bermuda Triangle

Central America

After kidnapping Crystal and Lockjaw, Diablo took over a Mayan Pyramid and attempted to overthrow the government of Terra Verde.

Starting a revolution in the tiny country of San Gusto, the Hate Monger's dreams of invading the United States and exposing the entire world to his hate ray were ended by the FF.

Antarctica

Antarctica was the location of the original undersea home of Atlantis, which was destroyed when an unnamed country tested an atomic weapon in the area.

Northern Atlantic

Hidden beneath the surface was the undersea kingdom of Atlantis, which was ruled by the Sub-Mariner.

The Northern Atlantic was also the location of the original island home of the Inhumans.

SOUTH AMERICA

South America

After living in the Northern Atlantic for thousands of years, climate changes forced the Inhumans to move the Great Refuge to the Andes Mountains.

Gazetteer

COMIC BOOK TITLES

A1—*Avengers* Vol. 1 (1963—96)
AA—*Avengers Annual*
AF—*Amazing Fantasy* (1962)
ASM—*The Amazing Spider-Man* Vol. 1 (1962—99)
CA—*Captain America* (1968—96)
D9—*Doom 2099* (1993—96)
FF—*Fantastic Four* Vol. 1 (1961—96, 2003—present)
F3—*Fantastic Four* Vol. 3 (1998—2003)
F5—*Fantastic Five* (1999—2000)
F9—*Fantastic Four 2099* (1996)
FFA—*Fantastic Four Annual*
H1—*The Incredible Hulk* Vol. 1 (1962—3)
JIM—*Journey Into Mystery* (1952—66)
LC—*Luke Cage, Hero For Hire* (1972—3)
MB—*Marvel Boy* (1950—51)
MC—*Marvel Comics* (1939)
MP—*Marvel Premiere* (1972—81)
MPF—*Motion Picture Funnies Weekly* (1939)
MTO—*Marvel Two-In-One* (1974—83)
NO—*Nova* (1976—9)
S9—*Spider-Man 2099* (1993—6)
SH—*The Savage She-Hulk* (1980—82)
ST—*Strange Tales* (1951—1968)
SW—*Marvel Super Heroes Secret Wars* (1984—5)
TH—*The Mighty Thor* (1966—96)
TT—*The Thing* (1983—6)
UXM—*The Uncanny X-Men* (1963—present)
W2—*What If* Vol. 2 (1989—98)

Afterword

It all comes down to family. If *Spider-Man* is a series that is rooted in responsibility, the *Fantastic Four* is all about family. A simple, average, all-American family that has breakfast together every morning but heads off to a hard day of challenging the unknown, saving the Earth, and fighting super-menaces. Okay, maybe this particular family doesn't always get along. Maybe Reed can be a tad patronizing. Maybe Ben and Johnny's squabbling does get out of hand. Hey, as the eldest of seven siblings, I can testify that families don't always get along. They bicker and storm off. They mooch off you during the holidays and borrow money they never intend to repay. There are times you really hate them and times you wouldn't survive without them. And all of that is mirrored in the Fantastic Four. Month after month, year after year, the FF shows us that nothing can beat a strong family. It will always find a way to survive. It just has to stick together.

I owe my career to those early issues of the *Fantastic Four*. If they hadn't sparked my imagination and rekindled my love of comics, I might have taken a different path and missed a lot fun.

Whenever I think of the *Fantastic Four*, Stan Lee and Jack Kirby immediately spring to mind. They created the characters and built the playground for the rest of us to enjoy. I salute all the many gifted writers, artists, and editors I have had the privilege to work with on the *Fantastic Four* over the years. You all belong to a special brotherhood and deserve a big *HOO-HA*!

The time has also come to thank Lindsay Fernandes, Laura Gilbert, Neil Kelly, and Alastair Dougall. They jumped in at the last moment to help me when a personal tragedy rendered me incapable of meeting my deadlines. This book would not exist without these people and I will always be in their debt for their work, their kindness, and their understanding. I am also grateful to Lisa Lanzarini and Nick Avery, who designed this book and kept taking my breath away with each exciting new layout.

While the original comics were my actual source material, I also relied rather heavily on the work of people like Mark Gruenwald, Peter Sanderson, Eliot Brown, Howard Mackie, Mark Bernardo, Bob Budiansky, Tom Brevoort, Eric Fein, and all the others who contributed to *The Official Handbook Of The Marvel Universe* (all three editions). The Internet has also become an amazing source of information. Fans of the FF will enjoy a visit to www.FFPlaza.com, The Fantastic Four Fluxion at www.shrublands.com/fluxion or the FF message board at www.comicboards.com.

Anyone interested in the FF should also look in on the current monthly comic books—*Fantastic Four*, *Marvel Knights 4*, *Ultimate Fantastic Four*, and any of the many limited series devoted to the team. The FF's earlier adventures have been reprinted in a variety of formats, from the *Marvel Masterworks* to the more economical *Essential* editions and dozens of trade paperbacks.

This book is dedicated to the memory of my beloved Patricia E., whose love, courage, and unflagging support propped me up for more than 35 years and still keeps me on track. I must also acknowledge Jimmy, Samantha, Bernie, Eddy, Tommy, Danielle, Christopher, Allison, Stephen, Meredith, Alexa, Andrew, Gerald, Carolyn, and the miracle we'll meet this May. They still give their grouchy old uncle a reason to remain a storyteller.

I would also like to express my gratitude to you, my reader, for just being there!

HOO-HA!

Tom D.

Index

Main entries are in **bold**

LONDON, NEW YORK, MUNICH,
MELBOURNE, AND DELHI

PROJECT EDITOR Lindsay Fernandes
SENIOR ART EDITOR Lisa Lanzarini
EDITORS Laura Gilbert and Neil Kelly
SENIOR DESIGNER Nick Avery
PUBLISHING MANAGER Simon Beecroft
ART DIRECTOR Mark Richards
CATEGORY PUBLISHER Alex Allan
PRODUCTION Rochelle Talary
DTP DESIGN Lauren Egan

First published in Great Britain in 2005 by
Dorling Kindersley Limited,
80 Strand, London WC2R 0RL

05 06 07 08 09 10 9 8 7 6 5 4 3 2 1

A CIP catalogue record for this book is available from the British Library

ISBN 1-4053-0996-2

Color reproduction by Icon Reproduction, London
Printed and bound in China by Leo Paper Group

Acknowledgments

DK Publishing would like to thank the following people:

Terry and Rachel Dodson for creating the cover art; Iain Wakefield, Jeff Poulin, and James
Hinton at Marvel Enterprises, Inc. for their help and support; Stan Lee for supplying the
foreword; Julia March for compiling the index; Kate Simkins for proof-reading; Sarah E.
Miller for editorial assistance; Jill Bunyan and Mika Kean-Hammerson for design
assistance; and Simon Mumford for supplying the world map.